Pilates

FOR RIDERS

Pilates
FOR RIDERS

Align your spine and control your core
for a perfect position

LINDSAY WILCOX-REID

J. A. ALLEN · LONDON

© Lindsay Wilcox-Reid 2010

First published in Great Britain in 2010

ISBN 978-0-85131-974-2

J. A. Allen
Clerkenwell House
Clerkenwell Green
London EC1R OHT

www.allenbooks.co.uk

J. A. Allen is an imprint of Robert Hale Limited

The right of Lindsay Wilcox-Reid to be identified as author of
this work has been asserted by her in accordance with the
Copyright, Designs and Patents Act 1988.

A catalogue record for this book is available from the British Library

Designed and typeset by Paul Saunders
Photographs by Bob Atkins,
except those on pages 6 and 7 by www.horsehero.com
Anatomical drawings by Carole Vincer
Alignment diagrams by Jennifer Bell
Edited by Marion Paull

Printed by New Era Printing Co. Limited, China

For more information about Lindsay Wilcox-Reid
and Equipilates tuition, please visit

www.equipilates.com

Contents

Foreword

by Laura Bechtolsheimer, international Grand Prix
dressage rider

I have been doing Pilates for over three years now and I am starting to feel the effects and benefits more and more. Although I have been riding internationally at Grand Prix level for five years now, my biggest successes came in 2009. I believe this strongly correlates with the level of Pilates I reached. Training hard with horses is all very well but if you are limited physically in strength or movement, there is only so much you can do. (If a horse is not worked through and supple, it cannot perform the movements. It is the same for us: the more supple and strong we are in the core, the better we can perform.) The longer I have been doing Pilates, the stronger my seat has become, which has enabled my hands to become completely independent of my seat.

Using Pilates exercises tailored for riding allows you to learn to switch on the 'right' muscles and turn off the 'wrong' ones, and to be aware of which you want to use. This has helped me to ride more of my big, strong horses without any backache or side effects. I also have more control over my body in the more difficult movements, so I can help my horses with their balance rather than hindering them. Being able to move and use different muscles independently, such

as my right leg in a change or pirouette, whilst my waist and upper body remain strong and stable, gives me an edge. Being able to rotate my upper body a fraction more to the inside, whilst the rest of me stays balanced and square, enables me to aid my horse more effectively in a canter pirouette or trot half-pass, because my bodyweight goes with the horse, yet my core is strong and my pelvis supple enough to absorb the horse's movement without rocking me at all.

Pilates is very satisfying; you can progress and feel the benefits very quickly. The longer you do it, the more you gain from it; you don't just reach a level and that's it. The progress is ongoing, so enjoy!

June, 2010

Acknowledgements

This list of thank-yous to all the people who have helped me acquire the understanding I have today and have facilitated the production of my thoughts into what I hope is a useful learning aid is rather vast, but here goes …

To my patient and supportive husband Chris, words cannot express how grateful I am for your emotional and practical support over the last nine years. My beautiful and precious boys Oliver and George, you mean the world to me.

I would like to thank my parents who in their very different ways helped me utilise my thirst for knowledge and determination to follow the career path I chose. Mum – your commitment to improving is a source of inspiration, as well as occasionally frustration (!) to me. I take great satisfaction from any of the light-bulb moments for which my input has been partly responsible. Dad, I really hope this helps you understand what I do, how I do it and why.

To Dennis, for believing in my dream and helping to make my vision a reality. Your support means a lot and I hope you feel the product is one to be proud of.

To Lisa Brooke for your fabulously elegant modelling skills and patient organisation of my scatterbrain. A loyal and close friend for (gulp) nearly fifteen years. How the time flies – your artwork is as beautifully presented as you!

To Chris Gratton – such a natural rider and yet so unassuming. A talented Pilates teacher with a gift for making things look effortless; your modelling of the studio shots is really appreciated. Thank you for your friendship over almost a decade.

To Judy Peck – a dedicated, considerate and thinking rider and a thoroughly lovely person. You are a constant source of useful information and advice. Thank you for embracing Equipilates and making it part of your life and your riding. I am very grateful for your modelling and your mint-dispensing skills!

To Angela Weiss, thank you for showing me another way – your knowledge and understanding of intelligent training inspired me to want to be the best teacher I could be.

To Pat Jenkins, your passion for teaching precision Pilates in its purest form, and your confidence in my abilities, have totally changed my life, and the lives of many I have worked with (human and equine), since first arriving at your studio.

To Steph Cooper – thank you for your enthusiasm and utterly useful solutions. You have shown me when to strip all the layers of analysis back to the most simple and amazing feeling – having fun and dancing with my horses.

To Phil Greenfield – your understanding of the human body on the deepest level has inspired me to open my eyes and my approach to teaching. To Jo, for Trinni.

To Lesley Gowers – your enthusiasm for this project coupled with horsey and Pilates expertise has made *Pilates for Riders* a work to be proud of.

To Bob Atkins – thanks for your patience and skill in producing amazing photos in such chilly conditions (and that was just the Pilates shots!).

Last, but most certainly not least, to my greatest teachers, levellers and friends – all the horses I have owned and ridden. Those who hold a very special place in my heart deserve a special mention – Ruskin (Goodwill), who knows what we could have achieved if I had known then what I know now; Boo, a genuinely wonderful soul whose generosity and kindness is humbling, a true friend; Trinni, my horse of a lifetime, the most powerful, opinionated yet amazingly talented horse I have ever had the privilege to ride. You are my true match in temperament and attitude to life, a total reflection of me. I respect your spirit as I do my own – together we will go forward, as partners.

Introduction

If you are anything like me, you may well be considering scanning through these first few pages quickly and then flicking straight to the nitty-gritty of the exercise section. I would make a plea now that, having invested in the purchase price of the book, you spend the time reading it in its entirety and in the order in which it is written to gain the maximum benefit. There are many exercises and techniques to experiment with throughout the chapters, and you will find it helpful to work through them before starting the Pilates programme. Whether you are a total newcomer to core stability and postural alignment work, a seasoned Pilates practitioner or riding professional, I hope the ideas and approach presented in this book will offer you a fresh perspective on how the rider can influence the horse and vice versa.

The Zen proverb 'When the pupil is ready to learn, the teacher will appear' really sums up how I came to find Pilates on my equestrian journey. I had trained several of my own horses to medium level dressage, but was simply unable to progress any further. I took pride in the fact that I was generally thought of as a decent rider – a 'strong', 'positive', 'get any sort of horse going' type of rider – and was committed to reaching a higher level of competitive dressage with the horse I owned at the time. He had been given to me after hospitalising his previous owner several times, a nervous lady who was most mismatched with him since she was the antithesis of strong or positive. He was a very stubborn and opinionated horse who simply would not move had my determination wavered. He competed under the name of Goodwill, which was a standing joke because he was one of the most ungenerous and awkward horses I have ever ridden. I absolutely adored him and he taught me a huge amount. Perhaps his breeder had a dry sense of humour!

We had done fairly well up to elementary level, qualifying for various regional championships, but once the requirements of the tests included more challenging lateral work, such as half-pass, full extensions of the trot and canter and, most notably, flying changes, I simply couldn't seem to get the horse to progress. In the case of flying changes, I couldn't get him to perform them at all. To say we reached a plateau is something of an understatement. I am a perfectionist and will repeat exercises *ad infinitum* in the quest for betterment, but the more time I dedicated to trying to improve, the more stuck I felt. Having spent a considerable amount of money on the best training, saddles, bits, physiotherapy treatment, massage pads and health care for him, I applied myself with renewed vigour each day with plans, strategies and training tips. The more effort I put in to riding and training him, the less he reciprocated, and schooling grew to be very disenchanting for both of us. The horse's work seemed to get progressively worse until he finally decided that all this was not in his contract, and resigned as my potential advanced dressage horse.

Eventually, I took the heartbreaking decision to sell him to someone who wanted to do a variety of activities, including hacking and jumping, while I found a 'better one' on the advice of my trainer at the time. As a strong and determined rider, they said, I really should have a better horse. So, a 'better horse' was found, bought and trained from just backed to medium level by me, where, to my surprise, we plateaued abruptly. Half-pass was a struggle, and the flying changes I was doubly determined and confident I would achieve failed to appear. Increasing my already strong aids – more leg, more seat and more hand on my kind, generous and willing-to-please horse – yet again seemed rather like a lot of hard work. The classical dressage ideals I had always aspired to seemed so far away.

Finally, after I had come in from a lesson with spur marks on the horse's sides from leg, leg and more leg, and little blisters on one side of the horse's mouth, I knew that this way of riding was absolutely and most definitely unacceptable. I discussed my frustrations with my trainer, and questioned whether using so much strength was necessary. I was told yes it was. I cannot lay the blame at the trainer's door, because watching me it was not particularly obvious quite how much body strength I was using. In any case, the instructors were simply passing on to me what they had been taught by some of the most renowned and respected international trainers in the country. I now understand that all too often trainers, unfortunately, just do not know enough about how much rider position affects the way of going of the horse – it is not currently a requirement of any of the equestrian teaching qualifications in this country to learn basics of human anatomy and biomechanics. When working with two beings as a partnership, one has to wonder why half of the team's athletic development is neglected.

A chance meeting with highly talented and knowledgeable trainer Angela Weiss (an international Grand Prix rider and para squad coach) was my first step on a new and enlightening path. Angela watched me warm up during my first lesson with her, and asked my mother incredulously, 'Does she always ride this *strongly*?' 'Erm … yes?' replied my mum quizzically. She knew how I had been taught and how much I had been praised for riding so positively. During the lesson – the first of many that took place over almost four years – Angela explained to me that the reason why I had not been able to achieve a proper half-pass or flying changes on this horse, the one before that and the ones before that was not because I needed a 'better one'. It seems so obvious now (hindsight is a wonderful thing), but I hadn't looked at myself; the constant plateau was because I needed to be a better rider.

My position was crooked, to the extent that to compensate for the weight aids I was unaware that my seat was giving the horse, my legs and arms had to work so hard that the tension and 'holding' strength within them had completely jammed my body. The harder I tried, the more crooked the pattern grew as my aids became stronger and stronger in their application. I was shocked to find that, when asked to focus on subtler detail in terms of balance and alignment of the horse, I struggled to use my body properly on a 20 metre circle – straight lines were even worse. Angela introduced me to a new feeling – doing much less, allowing time to receive feedback from the horse instead of applying aids before, and keeping them on long after, they were necessary. This way of riding was more precise and more enjoyable. Giving myself and my horse this time to process information opened up the sensation of 'feel' – something I had been missing when I was so busy talking with my body and not doing any listening.

After the lesson I realised that the issues that Angela had noticed were not random oddities. My seat was twisted and not level, while my upper body was not level and twisted in the opposite direction! My body seemed to be stuck in the same posture that I had used as a cellist. Throughout my teenage years I had practised for hours and hours each day, working on difficult virtuoso pieces and concertos, following my ambition to be a concert cellist. I had travelled to London frequently from the age of fifteen for lessons with two of the world's finest teachers, the late William Pleeth OBE (tutor of Jacqueline du Pre) and the international soloist Felix Schmidt. After studying at the Royal Academy of Music's junior department and later for a time at Birmingham Conservatoire, I totally lost confidence in my abilities when I failed to reach the televised rounds of the BBC Young Musician of the Year competition. Shortly after that I made the decision to follow a different path, a career with my other passion in life, which was horses. Although I had barely touched my cello for four or five years by the time I had that lesson with Angela, the patterns in my body had clearly been well established and were as strong as ever.

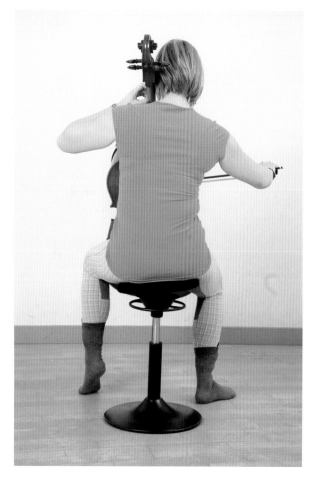 

Hours spent practising the cello each day 'set' me into a posture with a flattened lumbar curve in my spine, tilted upper body and head, rounded and elevated shoulders and uneven weight distribution.

Being a determined and dedicated sort of person, I set about the process of trying to rid my body of the crookedness that I had drummed into it for so long and so hard. I had previously had chiropractic treatment and sports massage, and had tried the Alexander Technique to try to release the tension that had plagued me while playing music as well as riding. This was not nervous tension but the result of using an unnecessary amount of strength in any task. Getting my body to do less felt odd and more than a little tricky. Angela made me aware that my body, and how I was using it on the horse, was having much more of an effect – and not necessarily a positive one – than I had previously realised. After doing a little bit of postural awareness work with a Pilates teacher, I played around with some of the techniques while I was riding and the instant improvement in the way of going of my horse whet my appetite to learn more.

Over a period of time I observed riders at different levels from novice to advanced dressage competitors working with Angela and other trainers. It became increasingly apparent that the horse's body was the mirror of the rider's, and vice versa – and usually not in the way that the rider intended. Both elements of the partnership, in the majority of cases, showed exactly the same alignment patterns. For instance, if the right side of the horse's body was shorter than the left, a glance upwards showed the same fault with the rider. If a rider was struggling to use her left leg effectively, the left side of the horse's body would be abandoned to its own devices, with either the left hind leg or the left shoulder (depending on quite how the rest of the rider's body was aligned) lacking the necessary support.

As a trainer myself, I knew that horses have crooked bodies with their own alignment patterns, and they favour one side for support more than the other, just as we are right-handed or left-handed. I realised that in some cases, the horse was drawing the rider into his crooked pattern because, when dismounted, the rider showed a completely different alignment pattern. In every case where riders are made aware of how their body either draws the horse into their own postural pattern, or is drawn into the horse's crookedness, major changes can be made in terms of achieving the next level in riding. By that I don't particularly mean increased dressage scores, cleaner jumping technique or a faster round – although those aspects are definitely a result of more body awareness – but, rather, more 'feel'.

For me, this was Pandora's box well and truly opened. The vision of Joseph Pilates, his ethos and the ability of his exercises to recondition the human body had captured my imagination. I decided that both for my own development and to enable me to teach riding to the very highest standard, I would train to be a qualified teacher of classical Pilates. Having successfully completed the course at the Pilates Advanced Training School in Milton Keynes, I became the first British Dressage trainer to hold a professional Pilates teaching qualification, and I now wonder how I managed to teach anybody anything about riding at all before I found Pilates! While continuing to research the biomechanics of the human body and the dynamics of the trainer/rider/horse relationship, I teach a large number of riders in the studio, on my lunge schoolmasters, and on their own horses. My aim is to make complex concepts understandable and accessible for riders at every level, whether their passion is hacking at the weekend or competing at international level. I fully embrace the Pilates approach to life, applying the principles not only while practising the exercises but every time I ride my horses, who remind me constantly why I am inspired by, and passionate about, my Equipilates teaching.

Chapter 1

Pilates Principles for Life

Pilates develops the body uniformly, corrects wrong postures, restores physical vitality, invigorates the mind and elevates the spirit.

JOSEPH PILATES

Pilates is a series of exercises designed to help your body to function better. Unlike many other types of exercise, it focuses on working your body from the inside out. Concentrating firstly on strengthening the deep abdominal muscles that support your spine, the exercises then work progressively on all of your other muscles, strengthening weak ones and stretching tight ones. Over time, and through the application of these exercises to specific postural problems, correct muscle balance can be restored, promoting symmetry front to back and left and right. Other benefits include increased mobility, flexibility and strength, improved circulation and lymphatic drainage, reduction in posture-related aches and pains, and lower stress levels.

A brief history

The Pilates method of exercise was developed by Joseph Pilates in the early twentieth century. Born in Germany in 1880, to Greek parents, Joseph was a sickly child, who suffered from rheumatic fever, rickets and asthma. After an intensive course of meditation, yoga and exercise, following the ethos of the ancient Greeks and Romans, his health improved dramatically – so much so that he became highly accomplished in boxing and skiing, and by the age of 14, he was also a skilled gymnast. As a young man, he is believed to have joined a group of Chinese acrobats in a travelling circus, and then in 1912, aged 32, he moved to England, where he boxed professionally and taught self-defence – to members of the police force among others.

At the onset of the First Word War, Pilates was interned, along with other German nationals who were residing in the United Kingdom at the time. He spent a year at a camp in Lancaster and, while he was there, started to develop a series of exercises, to be performed on mats, with the aim of building essential strength and flexibility. His idea of a combination of mental focus, controlled breathing and specific movements of deep muscles within the abdomen to support the spine and promote core stability was new, and his exercise regimen quite different from anything available at that time. Pilates' extensive study of anatomy and biomechanics meant that, while focusing firstly on the core muscles, he was able to tailor the movements to target either strengthening or stretching virtually every muscle in the human body.

During the latter part of the war, Pilates was transported to the Isle of Man to work as a hospital orderly. There he found patients, some disabled and bed-ridden, attempting to recover from injuries sustained in battle and during enemy internment, as well as disease. Drawing on the knowledge of strengthening muscles to aid recovery that he had gained as a child, he began to work with these patients, carefully and systematically moving limbs to help restore function. With the encouragement of the hospital medical staff, who had noticed shortened recovery times in these patients, Pilates continued to develop his theories. He made a piece of equipment using springs from old hospital beds to provide progressive resistance and bear weight. Later known as the 'Plié machine', this helped him to apply the principles that he had already begun to develop at Lancaster to those patients who were not physically fit enough, or at an appropriate point in their rehabilitation, to attempt the full movements.

After the war was over, Pilates returned to Germany where he worked with the Hamburg police, and his continually developing exercises and equipment attracted the interest of professional dancers. However, when the German Army began to take notice and tried to insist that Pilates train the troops, he found he had no desire to make his techniques available to them and, in 1923, emigrated to America. There, he and his wife Clara – who overcame her chronic arthritis by practising her husband's exercises – set up a studio in New York's Eighth Avenue, the heart of the dance community, where he continued to develop the exercise equipment that can be found in many studios throughout the world today. The studio, Pilates and his methods quickly became renowned for increasing strength, balance and flexibility as well as aiding rehabilitation when dancers injured muscles and joints.

Before his death in 1967, Joseph Pilates trained several 'master teachers' to continue his work. This is his legacy. His methods have been embraced all over the world, not only by dancers, actors, singers and athletes in many sports, but also by members of the medical and healthcare professions. Doctors and physiotherapists refer patients suffering from chronic conditions, as well as for injury rehabilitation, to teachers of the Pilates method.

Pilates is taught, either with the use of the studio equipment Joseph Pilates developed (this is usually on a one-to-one basis) or on yoga-type mats on the floor, through his original series of 34 exercises, often referred to as 'classical' Pilates. Proper execution of these mat-based exercises in the way that Joseph intended is probably limited to professional dancers, gymnasts or serious devotees of the technique, but all the exercises can be modified in many different ways so that virtually anybody at any level of fitness can benefit from practising them. Pilates can help sufferers from back pain, since the exercises present a low-impact but highly effective way to mobilise the body while providing muscular support to the spine by focusing on strengthening the deep abdominal muscles. Infinite variations of movement mean that a workout can be gentle, for a person of low physical fitness or in rehabilitation from injury, while being effective enough to improve body function. Workouts can also be very challenging, for the person who is already fit or using the techniques to help improve sports performance.

Why is Pilates good for riders?

The 'go for the burn' approach to fitness – pumping iron in the gym, or running for hours on a treadmill – can offer health benefits, if you have the time or inclination to do either! But the value of these activities in terms of how well your efforts transfer to the saddle, unfortunately, is fairly low. Pilates focuses on developing the skills needed to become a competent and effective rider – good alignment, core stability, flexibility and balance as well as self-awareness through a good mind/body connection. These are attributes possessed by élite riders – some display them naturally, through good luck, while others have to work hard to acquire them. For those of us not naturally blessed, regular practice of Pilates exercises can go a long way towards redressing the balance.

Working with, and riding, horses is an inherently dangerous activity; I am sure you have sustained at least one, if not multiple, injuries in your riding career, whether that is having your foot stamped on, or being thrown off at high speed. Recovery and rehabilitation from physical damage can be greatly assisted by practising Pilates exercises. Injuries, whether broken bones or soft tissue damage, can also have a dramatic impact on alignment and core strength and Pilates can help with this, too. Even a previous ankle sprain, perhaps sustained years ago, can cause your body to start loading differently!

Our bodies are put under strain not only by actually riding but also by all the extras – mucking out, then lifting and wheeling heavy barrows, heaving bales of hay, straw and shavings, carrying water buckets, being nearly pulled over by a horse spooking at a hedgerow monster. Riders have a tendency to extreme stoicism and tend to battle on through discomfort, seeking help from a doctor/chiropractor/osteopath only when they either can't ride any more or pain progresses to a point where they are severely limited in their ability to ride or care for their horse. Convincing riders that suffering in silence is unnecessary and there is no need to live with pain is a perpetual struggle. Regular Pilates practice helps to reduce risk of future injury by increasing stability, flexibility and balance, which may not prevent your foot being stamped on, but it should reduce the likelihood of you falling off!

The principles of Pilates

These should be applied not only while you are actively practising the exercises, but integrated into how you approach your everyday routine. The benefits gained from doing so, and the improvements in how your body moves and functions, will be reflected in other areas of your life.

- Relaxation

- Alignment

- Breathing

- Centring

- Flowing movement

- Focus

- Control

- Precision

- Stamina

All of the principles are interconnected – they depend upon, and are affected by, each other. It's a little bit like the 'scales of training', the building blocks for the training of the horse – rhythm/relaxation, suppleness, contact, impulsion, straightness, collection. Although each principle is important, you will probably find that you need to concentrate on one in particular in order to apply another. For instance, if you are not relaxed, or breathing correctly, flowing movement may well elude you. Moving with control and precision is difficult if the body is not correctly centred. The quality of performance, and benefit gained from any Pilates exercise, can be increased by revisiting and applying all of these principles.

Relaxation

Pilates perspective: Awareness of tension within the body/mind and how to release it is an important part of practising Pilates correctly. You want tone, not unnecessary tension, within your muscles. Unnecessary tension in muscles or muscle groups has an impact on your alignment.

Riding perspective: Tension held generally within the mind or body inhibits flexibility and ease of movement. Clear communication with your horse becomes more difficult when signals are muddled through tension. Tautness within certain areas of your body restricts the freedom of your movement, and limits how freely your horse can move underneath you, and may be interpreted by him as an instruction to reduce his movement.

Alignment

Pilates perspective: Good alignment helps your whole body and all the systems within it – circulatory, nervous, endocrine, lymphatic – to function properly.

Riding perspective: You need to be aligned as correctly as possible while riding in order to communicate clearly with your horse. Alignment is included in the Equipilates infinity cycle – see Chapter 2 for discussion of its effect on your horse and how to improve it.

Breathing

Pilates perspective: Breathing the Pilates way – full and wide into the sides and back of the ribs – helps to strengthen the abdominals as well as energising the body and clearing waste products.

Riding perspective: Proper use of breath ensures that you do not inadvertently block flowing movement within your own, or your horse's, body. Breathing technique is also included in the Equipilates infinity cycle – see Chapter 3 for a detailed analysis.

Centring

Pilates perspective: This means bringing your attention to the area between your pubic bone and ribs. Creating a 'girdle of strength' by using your deep abdominal and low back muscles helps to support your spine. Centring ensures you perform the exercises as intended by Joseph Pilates, working from the inside to the outside.

Riding perspective: On board a horse, there is a lot of movement to contend with and you need to be centred in order to maintain good alignment and spinal support. In order to appear still and balanced on any moving object, you must not remain static but move at exactly the same rate as that object. Centring enables you to do that while riding. Being able to use toned abdominal muscles helps you to resist movement forces generated by the horse, which otherwise may cause you to be left behind the motion, too far in front of it, or thrown to the left or right. Centring is the third principle in the trinity of infinity cycle (see Chapter 4).

Flowing movement

Pilates perspective: Moving with flow helps your body to be free of tension, stiffness and mechanical action. Joseph Pilates studied animals at liberty, including horses. He was fascinated by the fluidity, ease and grace with which they moved, along with their controlled strength and power. He wanted people to exhibit those same qualities, to reawaken the potential for easy and graceful movement that we have naturally as children but so often lose as we get older. Modern lifestyles keep us fairly static, and most of us spend too much time sitting down.

Riding perspective: The attributes that horses possess naturally and exhibit freely when playing in the field are those most riders seek to experience when backing and training them. If you do this sympathetically and correctly, you can teach your horse to offer you his innate grace, athleticism and power when you ride him. The most beautiful partnerships to watch are those where horse and rider seem to be working as one, the flow of communication between them seemingly telepathic, their bodies moving together like two dancers, undisturbed by any jarring or stilted action.

Focus

Pilates perspective: The ability to focus on individual parts of your body is important to gain maximum benefit from the exercises. Focusing on activating particular muscles or muscle groups, while keeping others released and soft, is called isolation.

Riding perspective: Isolating sections of your body enables you to apply aids independently while keeping the trunk stable. For instance, you must be able to apply leg or hand aids without disturbing the balance of your seat, and seat aids without disturbing the position of your legs or arms. Communicating certain requests to the horse requires you to move the upper trunk independently of the lower trunk, or the lower trunk independently of the upper trunk. Precision isolation of particular muscles is necessary to perform such actions as the half-halt.

Control

Pilates perspective: Each Pilates exercise should be executed with awareness of muscular control in every part of the body.

Riding perspective: By having greater control over how your body moves and its positioning, you are far more able to influence your horse's balance and movement. Having control over your body means you can move, and aid your horse, with precision.

Precision

Pilates perspective: Focussing on how different parts of the body are moving, whilst being aware of the body as a whole, means that specific muscles and groups of muscles can be isolated for stretching or strengthening at any point as appropriate within the exercise.

Riding perspective: Precise movements of your body are important so that you can apply aids clearly and with a good sense of timing. Applying them speedily, and also removing them when they are no longer necessary, allows your horse to understand and react more responsively. It is also a more efficient use of energy and therefore less tiring for you.

Stamina

Pilates perspective: Stamina is required to build endurance strength into key muscles, particularly for spinal support.

Riding perspective: Have you ever seen somebody who visits the gym on a regular basis, or perhaps a bodybuilder with very defined arm muscles? They may be shopping at the supermarket or walking the dog and paying no attention to using their bodies in the way that they would do if lifting weights. However, the muscle tone is obvious, and you can see that their arms are strong, because they concentrate on strengthening those muscles when they are lifting weights. In the same way, you want to strengthen your abdominal, centring muscles so that they continue to support your spine even when you are not thinking about it. This is especially important when riding, because there are so many other things to think about at the same time. It's also important that the abdominal muscles carry on working, whether you are actively focusing on them or not, while you are doing all the extra jobs, including mucking out, pushing heavy barrows and lifting bales.

Thinking about and applying all of the Pilates principles every time you ride helps to improve the experience for both you and your horse. However, there are so many things to consider while riding that, realistically, it is probably easier and more practical to focus on the three major principles of alignment, breathing and centring – call it your riding ABC. I like to call it the 'trinity of infinity' because you need to keep revisiting each one in a constant cycle of awareness, an endless connection.

Chapter **2**

Trinity of Infinity – Alignment

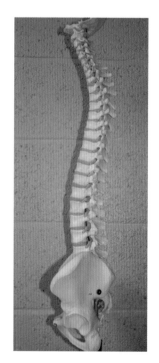

Gentle curves flow into one another to form the spinal column.

orrect alignment is imperative for your body to function at its best, and for you to be an effective and efficient rider. The old 'ear, shoulder, hip and heel' line taught in riding schools the world over has been universally adopted for a very good reason; we will explore exactly why in more detail later in the chapter.

Pilates exercises start by establishing what is referred to as 'neutral spine' as a base for all movement. Thereafter, correct alignment in terms of the placement of certain parts of your body in relation to others differs with each exercise, depending on the specific aims and objectives of the movement required. Neutral spine really describes not only your spine, but the alignment of your whole body. If you are in neutral spine it means that you are not displaying one of the postural extremes, such as a hunched or arched back, and that your skeleton (ear, shoulder, hip, heel) is primarily aligned to the line of gravity – vertical – taking into account the natural curves of your spine.

Your body is a fantastically well-designed piece of apparatus when it is working as nature intended. Your skeleton provides support, structure and protection for your vital organs. The well-aligned skeleton absorbs shock through the joints and bears the weight of your entire body. Bones are light but very strong. Deep muscles close to your spine work to keep you upright while others help you to move. They work in pairs and in teams – muscles have specific actions, with their partners having the exact opposite action, e.g. your biceps flex your elbow and your triceps straighten it. While your biceps are flexing or your triceps straightening, muscles in your shoulder are working to keep the top of the arm stable. When your muscles have completed an action, they return to a 'resting length', ready for action when you need them, and waiting patiently to be called upon.

This body's muscles are good team players. Movement is easy and regular in all directions as the muscle strength is evenly developed, front to back, side to side and inside to outside, that is from deep muscles to muscles nearer the surface. This body does not generally suffer from niggly aches and pains and the organs within it function well. The force of gravity – acting vertically downwards, and diametrically and equally opposed by the action of muscles surrounding the spine – is this body's friend.

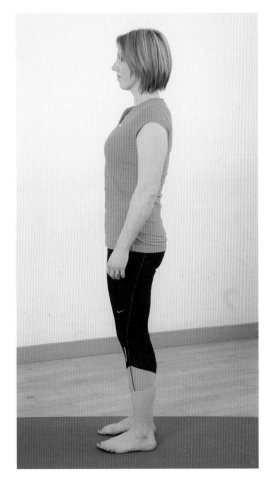

From the moment of birth, all the processes of learning movement – lifting your head, crawling, walking and balance – combine to help form the spine into an S shape. As babies explore new ways to use their bodies, their muscles develop evenly, giving flexibility in lots of directions – at that stage, life involves plenty of movement and then more movement, sleeping in between to recharge the batteries, and who sleeps more deeply and peacefully than a child?

As we grow into adulthood, generally speaking we move less and less, and the ways in which we do move become very repetitive, using the same or similar movement patterns day after day. We tend to get more mentally tired – as opposed to physically tired – than we used to, yet have less quality sleep as worries play on our minds. Modern lifestyles mean we spend long periods of time sitting – at a desk, in a car, in front of the television or computer screen. The human body functions at its best with regular and varied movement, which cannot be achieved while sitting down. If you work with horses, although active, you will be using the same muscle groups for the same actions every day, whether you are mucking out or riding several horses, or both. You may have had accidents or injuries in the past, which caused trauma to your body and altered the way you use it. To avoid causing yourself discomfort, you will stop using the injured part of your body and, in the process, overload other areas. This may be temporary, but can become a habit. Repetitive actions, such as carrying a child on the same hip or water buckets in one hand rather than the other, cause overloading. All of these things mean that certain muscles start to work very hard – those that keep you in a sitting position, for example, or squinting at your computer screen as you hunch over the keyboard, or throwing that muck up and over, twisting right to left, right to left, right to left. Gravity does its work, pulling you into crookedness.

above Sitting for long periods is not good for your alignment.

above right Repetitive movements can cause muscle imbalance.

Why is good alignment important for your riding?

Your position has a huge impact on the way your horse moves underneath you. Your spinal alignment influences every aspect of your riding, from where your legs are positioned on the horse's sides to how you can apply a half-halt aid. Poor alignment, together with a lack of stability and flexibility, affects how well you can absorb the horse's motion, for example in the sitting trot. If your weight is unevenly distributed, perhaps loaded forward or back of the vertical line of gravity, or you find it more difficult to turn one way compared with the other (or both of those things!), your body will be giving signals to the horse to move in a certain way, even if you aren't aware of it. Tiny deviations have an impact on how you and your horse work together. Almost all of the time, correcting rider alignment dramatically reduces the horse's apparent one-sidedness, and helps enormously with straightness issues, loss of bend or engagement in transition and contact problems.

Once these issues have become less troublesome, the genuine training needs of the horse become clearer to both trainer and rider – progress suddenly seems much more straightforward. Many riders spend a fortune on having their horses treated by a physiotherapist or chiropractor, and having their saddles checked and refitted regularly, and yet are unaware of the huge impact their own riding has on their horse's ability to move freely, and the effect it has on whether the treatment received will be effective in the long term. As one half of the partnership, it is just as important that your body functions to the best of its ability, to ensure that the money you spend on your horse's welfare is not wasted.

Professional riders, who may struggle with muscular aches or back pain from riding several horses per day, often find that, through progressively improving alignment and core support, they are able to ride for longer without soreness or loss of performance. Sore backs, shoulders and arms from exercising strong, leaning or difficult horses – or asking for the dreaded sitting trot on big moving horses – can make riding a chore, when it should be a pleasure. Tight hamstrings, hip flexors and contracted calf muscles can be aggravated by continually motivating lazy horses – stretching and lengthening those tight, short muscles may make leg aids more effective.

Understanding straightness and how to achieve it can help you to help yourself, and your horse, avoid pain, strain, biomechanical dysfunction and poor performance. The horse's 'straightness' in the scales of training is not gained by rigidly holding him in a shape, but is the result of the progressive suppling and strengthening of his body through the work you do with him to ensure flexibility and hind-leg support become equally available. If it is possible to work your horse evenly and easily both left and right, and have influence (through your position) on the flight path of each of his legs, controlling his shoulders and quarters to find straightness in the middle should not prove too difficult.

The route to human straightness works along the same lines. Just as your horse will not stop hanging on one rein unless he is shown some other way to balance and support himself, your body will not let go of its current postural pattern, with certain strong areas operating the whole mechanism, unless the pattern is reprogrammed. Stretching, releasing tension and manual manipulation of these workaholic muscles will often be effective only on a short-term basis, usually until you start performing a familiar action, when your workaholic muscles simply take over again and continue the cycle. For the release of excess tension or to maintain length in those overworked muscles, which have become too short and tight, it is necessary to strengthen the weak areas within the body in order that they may function as nature intended and relieve their counterparts from assuming too much responsibility. Muscles that remain in a stretched position, as well as muscles stuck in shortness, can cause you considerable discomfort.

The benefits of working in neutral

It is important to understand how your body alignment can influence the way your horse moves underneath you and vice versa. For working your horse on the flat, the optimum position for you to assume is neutral, with the curves of your spine in a correct relationship to one another, and on a vertical axis. Neutral is the base position from which you work in Pilates – the nature of the exercises means that if your body does not naturally assume a correct neutral alignment, progressive practice will help you to work towards developing and maintaining it. When the body is aligned to gravity, you can move in various directions, with neutral as the central point, to absorb the horse's motion with minimal disturbance of his balance. I must stress that you should not fix the body into a new position – good riding requires the spine to flex and extend through neutral, to flex equally each side of neutral and to rotate from neutral equally both ways. This is necessary to achieve fluidity with the oscillating motion of the horse's back in different paces.

Tension and stiffening have just as negative an effect on the horse as poor alignment does. They may even have more of an effect, by blocking his movement. 'Dynamic neutral' means that you can always recognise neutral as the central point of movement, and are able to return to it if you move, or are moved, away from it. In short, a neutral position in the saddle means that you have equally weighted seat bones, no part of your body is turned, shifted or tilted to the left or right, and your skeleton is weightbearing – so there is no excessive muscle tension. In neutral, aids are *not* being applied – it is the passive place to

return to after applying any aids, a place to harmonise with the horse. Every person's body is different, and responds in different ways to the stresses and strains we place upon it. If working in neutral is difficult or uncomfortable, that could be an indication of a postural or structural issue – some people, due to past injury, trauma or other physiological reasons, may never be able to achieve it. However, we can all work *towards* functioning in ideal alignment. Each step closer will pay dividends in both performance and communication between you and your horse.

The application of leg, seat and hand aids becomes muddled if your entire spine maintains a position other than neutral, partly due to the effect this has on the distribution of your weight. To apply an aid of any sort, remember it may be necessary to move out of neutral momentarily, but it is important to return to this central point so that aids do not remain on for too long since this makes them less effective. If a point other than neutral spine becomes the centre of movement, you are no longer aligned to gravity, which means you will struggle to maintain your leg position and contact, and clarity of communication through your seat. Therefore the axis of your spine should be vertical. Around this axis, the large bony structures of your pelvis, ribcage and head should be stacked level and square. From there, you can consciously choose to move any of these – for instance, rotating your ribcage to assist in turning.

Your leg and hand positions, and therefore your ability to use those aids with precision, are also affected by spinal alignment. The spine in neutral encourages a correct leg position with minimal effort – the legs drop down easily from the hip joint, helped by the force of gravity. If the spine or pelvis is tilted on to a backward axis, this tends to thrust the legs forwards. A small degree of backward tilt in the spine or pelvis means that to achieve that long, elegant leg position that dressage riders crave, the rider will always have to use just that little bit extra effort to get the legs underneath them. Sometimes riders who have previously tipped, or collapsed, forwards are constantly told to 'Sit back! Sit BACK!' and end

sequence Look how the rider's spine moves during the phase of a canter stride, but maintains neutral in the moment of suspension.

The spine on a marked backward axis has sent the legs forwards significantly.

The spine on a forward axis can result in the legs swinging back.

up taking the entire spine, probably still in its original C curve, backwards and rolling right onto the back of their bottoms. This in turn sends the legs forwards into a 'water-skiing' position and leaves the rider in a different, although still undesirable, alignment. The farther back the pelvis is tilted, away from neutral, the more difficult it is to maintain a correct leg position.

A slightly tilted or tipped forward spine may indicate nerves, in which case the legs may still be drawn forwards and up as the hip joint closes towards the foetal (fatal!) crouching position. However, the farther forwards the body moves, the farther back the legs will swing.

Often, with a positional fault of this kind, the entire spine doesn't need to move farther back – since this can result in a spine backward axis and legs forward pattern – but just the upper body. Spinal extension exercises, such as Headlight Dazzle, Dart, Swan, Single-leg and Double-leg Kick (see Chapter 9 Pilates Workout Exercise List), which strengthen the abdominals in a lengthened position and also the back muscles, help with this fault.

Here, just the upper body needs to realign.

Thinking about posture

So, how can you develop awareness of your postural patterns? More importantly, how can you adjust them? Imagine the large bony structures of your body as a stack of boxes – one box is your pelvis at the base of the stack, one box your ribcage and one box your head, and the spine is the central axis. Each of these boxes can shift forwards or backwards, tilt forwards or backwards, shift laterally, tilt laterally and rotate. Since muscles interact in groups and chains throughout the body, if one of your boxes is out of line, the others will move in order to keep some sort of balance so you don't fall over, although the altered stacking pattern may not be helpful in terms of how you sit on a horse.

Unconsciously applied weight aids

When you are riding, if your boxes are not stacked evenly, your body weight is likely to be concentrated over one side of the horse. As a general rule, horses follow the weight of the rider, making it one of your most powerful aids, which you need to use wisely. Incorrect use has all sorts of confusing effects, as well as possibly being detrimental to the horse's movement.

The horse 'wears' you on his back, a bit like you wearing a backpack – if the backpack is unevenly loaded, you keep moving around, trying to get the centre of the load in the middle of your back, to make it easier for you to carry. The horse does the same, but if the 'load' (you) is always over one side, he will always be drifting that way, following the weight aid you are giving, although you may not be aware of it. To you, this can feel like the horse is always falling out, favouring the outside, or inside, shoulder, or leaning on one rein, or is harder to turn or bend one way, or to move laterally.

If you are giving the horse an unintentional weight aid, you will have to use much more leg and hand on the corresponding side to override this than if your weight was central. Sometimes, on a young or particularly unbalanced horse, you may find yourself leaning in completely the opposite direction to the horse to try to counteract his loss of balance and return him to your intended line of travel – this can become something like a tug of war, with him leaning ever farther one way, and you the other. If you can break the cycle by going with him a little more instead of against him, it actually frees your leg to move him away from it more effectively.

below left An incorrect stacking pattern on a circle – the rider's pelvic box has slipped to the outside, altering her leg position. Her ribcage box has tilted and over-twisted – the whole of her body has grown longer on the right side and shorter on the left, encouraging the same pattern in the horse, who is falling badly through the outside shoulder.

below right The same incorrect stacking pattern from above.

Some stacking patterns may look fairly similar but cause the horse to react differently in his way of going. The pictures on page 34 show what trainers may identify as a 'collapsed hip' or 'dropped shoulder' but the effect on the horse is different in each one due to the load distribution – the different, and unintentional, weight aid being given. The stacking patterns in both photographs will probably result in the rider finding that bending the horse correctly to the left is difficult.

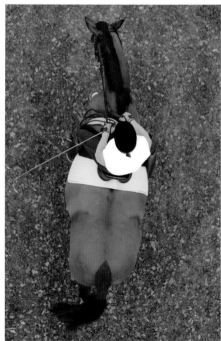

A correct stacking pattern on a circle – the rider's weight is evenly distributed and she is rotating her ribcage box in line with her intended line of travel. The horse has support in both reins and is in much better balance on the circle.

The same correct stacking pattern from above.

left-hand photo An incorrect stacking pattern in the leg-yield. The horse is following the rider's weight, which is loaded excessively to the right. The twisted upper body means that the rider has lost control of the horse's outside shoulder and cannot influence the hind legs properly. The horse has lost engagement, and the duo looks untidy and unbalanced.

right-hand photo A correct stacking pattern in the leg-yield. The rider is sitting centrally over the horse's spine and her legs are free to influence the angle and amount of crossing in the movement. The horse is balanced and shows much better engagement of the hind legs.

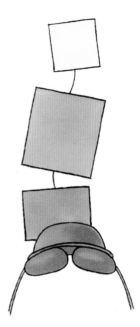

This is an interesting pattern. The rider's ribcage box is weighted a little to the left, while her pelvic box is weighted a little to the right. The slight movement of the boxes means that there is not an excess of load going in one direction more than the other, so the horse continues to move along a straight line of travel. However, the pattern is crooked because the horse aligns his shoulders to the left and pelvis to the right, like the rider's, and moves on three tracks, a bit like a shoulder-in.

Here we see a short right waist, lower right shoulder and unlevel seat as the rider's weight is concentrated over the left side of the horse. Depending on how the rider uses her leg and hand aids, the horse may fall through the left shoulder, with the rider finding it easier to bend the horse to the right but not to turn to the right. Alternatively, the horse may swing his quarters left, in which case the rider will find it difficult to control them because her left leg does not have a good contact with the horse.

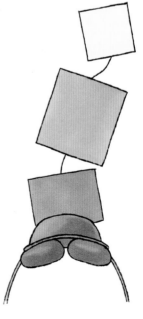

This picture also shows a short right waist, lower right shoulder and unlevel seat, but this time the rider's weight is concentrated over the right side of the horse. Again depending on how she uses her other aids to compensate, she may sense a 'motor-biking' feeling, i.e. that the horse is falling on to his right shoulder all the time and won't move well away from her right leg.

Consciously applied weight aids

From a vertical axis and stacked boxes, you can consciously apply a weight aid to ask your horse to move in the direction of the increased load. However, problems occur if you use a weight aid when you aren't balanced centrally to begin with. It is my belief that unless you are able to maintain a central position, the active use of weight aids is inappropriate. In the photos of the bay horse with the turquoise bandages I am riding Ticketyboo, working at medium level and therefore using fairly shallow angles for lateral exercises. The photo on page 46 shows even weight distribution in a correctly ridden movement. From this point on, as long as I maintain length in my spine and my sense of being centralised, and am able to return to it at any time, I may choose to move out of neutral a little in order to apply more of a weight aid to achieve steeper angles and greater bend.

Adopting 'neutral pelvis'

In order to start building your stack correctly, with a stable base, i.e. your pelvic box, you must be able to sit with your seat bones level and evenly weighted. This is neutral pelvis.

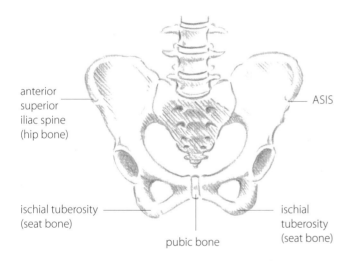

anterior superior iliac spine (hip bone)

ASIS

ischial tuberosity (seat bone)

ischial tuberosity (seat bone)

pubic bone

The pelvis from the front.

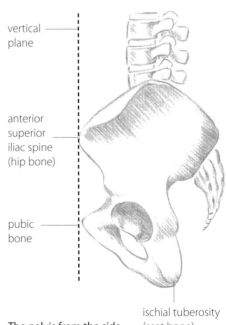

vertical plane

anterior superior iliac spine (hip bone)

pubic bone

ischial tuberosity (seat bone)

The pelvis from the side.

While sitting on your horse, allow your body to rock gently from side to side like a pendulum, and see if you can feel the pressure change from a bony lump in the left side of your bottom to a bony lump in the right side. If you can't feel the bony lumps, ask someone to hold your horse, and sit on your hands as you rock – this should make them more apparent. These are your seat bones, or ischial tuberosities, if you want to use the technical term. The seat bones are shaped a bit like rockers and you need to be sitting on the right part of the rockers to ensure the correct curvature of the lumbar spine. Too much or too little curve here limits your ability to absorb the shock of the horse's movement. Once you are sitting evenly on the bony lumps, you are in neutral in the forward-and-back plane of motion. This is what most people who have been to Pilates classes would think of when neutral is mentioned.

To find neutral pelvis while in the saddle, make your triangle as shown in the photographs below. Now imagine your pelvis is a bowl of water (see photographs and diagrams opposite).Without moving your upper body, tip your bowl of water forwards so the water spills out of the front of the bowl on to the pommel of the saddle. You will feel that your triangle is tilted, and your hip bones, rather than your pubic bone, are closer to the horse's ears.

Place the heels of your hands on your hip bones – the bony lumps at the top of your pelvis. The technical term for each of these is anterior superior iliac spine, or ASIS.

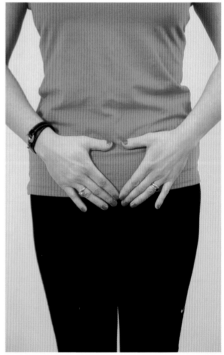

Place your index or third fingers on your pubic bone. This will be around the base of your zip line if wearing breeches or jodhpurs. Flatten your thumbs to your stomach to make a triangle shape.

Now tip your bowl backwards so that the water spills out of the back of the bowl on to the cantle of the saddle. You will feel that your triangle has tilted the other way, and your hip bones, rather than your pubic bone, are farther away from the horse's ears. Notice which of these directions feels easier. Neutral pelvis is when all three bones are on a vertical plane and your triangle is upright.

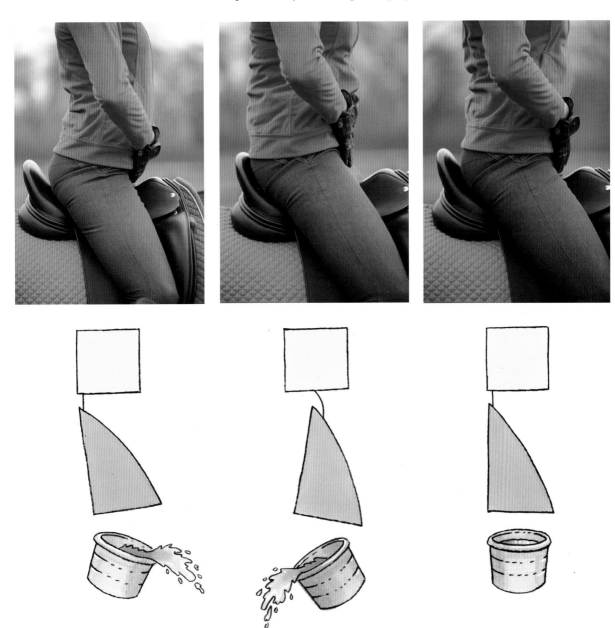

The pelvis in a forward tilt – water spills out of the front of the bowl.

The pelvis in a backward tilt – water spills out of the back of the bowl.

The pelvis is in neutral – the water is level in the bowl.

This may change the feeling of your seat bones. If you generally sit too far back on them, you may feel more towards your 'fork' and that the bones seem sharper, smaller or more pointed. This is because you are now sitting on a smaller surface area of the rockers. If you normally sit too far forward, with an excessive curve in the lumbar spine, you may feel slightly collapsed and flatter in your lumbar region, and the seat bones may feel bigger. This is because you are now sitting on a larger surface area. Depending on your position, you may need to think of arching or flattening your back. What is an appropriate instruction or visualisation for one rider is not necessarily correct for another who shows a different alignment pattern.

Awareness of your alignment and its effect on how your horse moves underneath you is the first step to improving how you work together. You must also be aware of how your horse's movement affects *you* in terms of balance and symmetry.

It is worth noting that although a person often stands on the ground in the same alignment – always with more weight on the right leg and the right shoulder lower than the left, for example – once that person gets on a horse and starts asking for certain movements, the pattern may change completely. You may stand with an arched back but roll on to your bottom when sitting on a horse and flatten your lumbar curve. So, although your alignment pattern when off the horse predisposes you to ride in a certain way, it is by no means fixed in stone. Your posture may change dramatically when you sit on your horse, and alter even more in movement.

You will probably display more than one alignment pattern during a single ride, depending on what you are asking of the horse. Each pattern alters the messages your body is giving to the horse about where and how to move. It also alters the feedback you receive from the horse. Men and women have structurally slightly different skeletons, and different levels of strength and flexibility. However, in terms of correct alignment the principles are the same, as are the muscle groups that work as you ride. Therefore I have not made any differentiation and the exercises are appropriate for both sexes throughout the book. You need to assess your postural patterns when dismounted as well as when riding, and the tips for self-assessment scattered throughout this chapter are there to help.

To be sitting in neutral pelvis, not only do your seat bones have to be level, the pelvis has to face straight forward, and not turn to the left or right. If your pelvis does turn one way, your legs will be placed on different areas of your horse's ribcage, making contact uneven and riding the horse straight, with equal control of both sides of his body, a struggle. A rider with a pelvic box pushed farther back on the left than on the right will often twist a saddle's cantle to the right and vice versa. Over time, this will affect the muscle development of the horse's back, and the saddle balance, too.

Often, riders will be unable to use one of their legs effectively, or keep it underneath them, because of a rotation of the pelvic box. This may be slight, or more obvious, as in the photograph below. It is logical to assume that if your hip is farther forward on one side, the leg will also be farther forward, and if you find that one leg is forward, you could try shuffling your seat bone farther back to see if it takes your leg with it. Plenty of riding manuals tell us 'inside hip forward to bring the leg forward' and vice versa, but this may not always work. While it holds true for highly trained riders – those who have studied at the great educational institutions of the Spanish Riding School or Cadre Noir and developed a very supple and elastic seat through endless hours on the lunge, for example – many riders have tight muscles in the hips and, in fact, the pattern is reversed. Depending on just which muscles in the hip, leg and lower back are being overused, an excessively forward leg position on one side can actually be exacerbated by the seat being too far *back*.

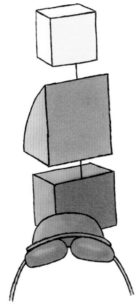

This rider has rotated her whole body to the left – look how the left seat has pushed the cantle of the saddle over to the right of the horse's spine.

Remember, the basic neutral position – when the pelvis rolls, or moves, back, the legs go forwards; when it rolls forwards, the legs go back. If you have one leg that perpetually moves forwards and won't stay back underneath you, try rolling forwards from the back of your seat bone to point your hip bone towards the horse's opposite ear – you should feel a stretching down or pulling sensation at the top of the front thigh as it releases downwards more vertically. So for the rider in the picture above, because her pelvis is twisted to the left, her left seat bone is farther back on the saddle than is the right one. She has rolled on to the back of the left seat bone, bringing the left side into a backward tilt and thrusting the left leg forwards. By asking her to roll forwards on to the correct part of her left seat bone and point her left hip towards the horse's right ear, she can bring the left side of the pelvis into neutral, releasing the hip. As the seat is corrected, she will find it easier to keep the left leg in position on the horse. Making a conscious effort to stretch the left leg back towards the horse's quarters while she is riding will also help to position the hip and seat bone correctly.

What if you can't seem to find equal weight in your seat bones?

A common frustration with riders is that even though they are aware that they should be able to feel equal weight in their seat bones, when they focus on it, they always seem to sense one more than the other. This can be caused by lateral shifting, as well as rotation, of the pelvic box, which can put you on one section of one seat bone and a different section of the other – the sensations of weight can feel different if you are not sitting on the same point on each seat bone. If you can always feel, let's say, your left seat bone more than your right, it could be that your weight has shifted over to the left and your left seat bone is lower. In which case, shuffling slightly over to the right and lowering your right seat bone into the saddle should help. Check your zip line to assess whether you are now centrally aligned. (See self-assessment checks on page 52.)

Sometimes you can be more aware of one seat bone if it is jammed against the saddle, when in fact the load of your bottom has shifted the other way, leaving the seat bone on that side floating somewhat in midair. If adjusting your position as described above hasn't levelled the seat bones, try slightly shuffling

Here I can feel more pressure on the right seat bone, although you can clearly see the load of my seat is over to the left.

your bottom *towards* the side that feels 'sharper' to you – and see if you become aware of the missing side as you bring it back into contact with the saddle.

The ribcage box

Many riders and trainers are aware of the importance of correct positioning of the pelvis and the placement of the seat bones, but the ribcage and its influence is mentioned far less frequently. Although the placement of each box effects the placement of the others, it does not always follow that because your pelvis may be in the right place, the rest of your spine will also be in ideal alignment. We therefore need to look at the other boxes and address the stacking of each one individually. Once all of the boxes are correctly stacked, the spine may move as a whole, in balance and fluidity. While riding, you may need to focus on one particular box (the primary influence) in order to help the rest of the boxes stack properly. This could be any one of them – the pelvic, ribcage or head box.

Just as horses will follow the weight of the pelvic box if it is loaded to one side, they will also follow the weight of the ribcage. The ribcage box can turn, shift laterally andtilt laterally – which can give the appearance of one shoulder being lower than the other – and tilt up or down. If the ribcage box is shifted forwards or backwards, or tilted up or down, your ability to maintain a steady and even contact is compromised, due to the position of the shoulder blades (scapulae). The muscles that help to maintain correct stacking of the ribcage box on top of the pelvic box, also work to stabilise the shoulder blades. Your rein contact with the horse's mouth is rooted at the scapulae, and modified at the elbow and in the hand. If the arm does not have a stable base from which to work, i.e. a correctly placed shoulder blade, there is little fine control over its movement, and contact can easily become too hard, not positive enough, intermittent and inconsistent. The arms can become fixed due to the overuse of upper shoulder and neck muscles, which causes tension and discomfort. Also, if the ribcage box is not properly positioned, the horse can pull you forwards more easily, or pull your arms too straight.

A useful visualisation

An effective way to keep your ribcage box properly stacked and your spine well aligned is to visualise your chest as a pair of headlights! Where would your headlights be pointing as you read this? On dipped beam, probably, as most people's tend to be a lot of the time. When you ride, think of your headlights being on full beam, to help you sit upright and not hunched or tipped forward. Always pointing your headlights in the direction you want to go is a helpful aid in turning your upper body correctly on corners and circles. On a straight line, do they shine straight ahead, or off to one side?

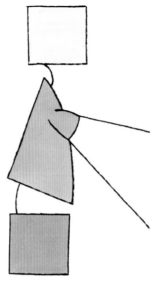

Here we see the ribcage tilted down at the front, with the headlights definitely on dipped beam! This is an extremely common posture, from which it's easy to be pulled or tipped forwards. Riding in this pattern makes it difficult to maintain an elastic contact, with bend in the elbow – the muscles in the upper shoulders and neck can feel sore, especially after riding a strong horse. Practising spinal extension exercises, such as Headlight Dazzle, Swan and Dart, will help with this.

Here we see the ribcage tilted up at the front – being told constantly to sit up with your shoulders back can cause this military, rather braced pattern. The headlights are dazzling far too much. The mid-back muscles are working too hard, and tension may be felt in the back, between or below the shoulder blades as well as lower down. For help with this pattern, practise spinal flexion exercises, in particular the Bow, which recruits the upper abdominals to lower the sternum and lengthen the back muscles.

Here we see the ribcage has shifted backwards. Projecting the sternum horizontally forwards, towards the pommel of the saddle, helps to correct this pattern. Imagine Kate Winslet standing at the bow of the ship, arms thrown wide, in the trailer for the film 'Titanic'. The Chest Opener and spinal-extension exercises Headlight Dazzle, Swan and Dart are useful.

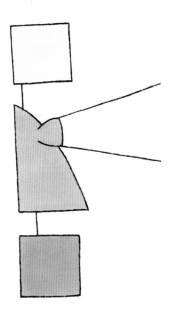

Here the ribcage is neutral – the rider's bra strap is horizontal all the way round her trunk and her headlights are level. Ladies, it is well worth investing in a properly fitted sports bra – subconsciously, or even consciously, trying to hide your bust as you ride impacts on the correct alignment of your spine.

Tilted ribcage, lateral shift and rotation

A ribcage that tilts down on one side often goes with a pelvic box that slips or shifts, but not always. If you happen to glance down and see that one of your hands is carried lower than the other, this can indicate that the ribcage is lower on the side of the lower hand. A ribcage that is constantly turned to one side invites the horse to drift or fall out on the opposite side and can make it feel as though the horse is very easy to bend in the direction of the ribcage rotation, but much more difficult the other way. The rider in the photograph below feels that the horse hangs on the left hand and falls through the right shoulder a bit when on the left rein, but won't stretch into the left hand when travelling on the right rein.

Notice the rider's rotation and collapse. Her ribcage is twisted to the left –you can see much more of the right hand than the left, and her left elbow is bent while the right is almost straight. The left side of her waist has shortened, and the right side has lengthened, allowing the same thing to happen with the horse.

In one sense, it is fairly irrelevant which member of the partnership draws the other into misalignment, because, in any case, it is the rider's responsibility to recognise the issue and take corrective action. The rider in the photograph above can improve her alignment by learning to activate her waist muscles (right obliques), to turn her ribcage to the right (in order to centralise it) and shorten the right waist. This will balance the ribcage better on top of her pelvis, give her right side more security and support and prevent the horse drifting through the right shoulder. It will also allow some lengthening and release of the left side, giving room for the horse to stretch into it and reduce the feeling of rein-contact imbalance. Keeping her right elbow, in particular, close to her waist will help her to maintain the correct feeling.

This alignment pattern is typical of a rider who is constantly told to 'turn your shoulders more!' but doesn't have the rotational ability in the right part of the spine to do so while maintaining correct alignment. Insufficient rotational flexibility in the thoracic part of the spine, means that, instead of turning from the centre, the rider can achieve the required turn only by trying to push the outside shoulder farther and farther forwards, ending up overly recruiting one side of the obliques and flexing the spine too much laterally. This shortening of the waist may result in what looks like a collapsed hip, which is easily spotted by a trainer or observer. Otherwise, it may result in a lateral shift of the ribcage, which, unfortunately, will probably not be correctly identified as such.

Lateral shifts are more difficult than other patterns to spot. Often trainers will see something that doesn't look quite right in a rider's position, but are unable to work out quite what is wrong, since the seat and the shoulders seem level. Look at the half-pass picture below and note the sideways shift of the ribcage. Lateral shifting of the ribcage to the outside puts weight towards the outside shoulder of the horse, making his neck seemingly easier to bend, but his shoulders harder to turn or control because they are busy drifting underneath the weight of the rider's ribcage and outside seat. The pelvic and ribcage boxes need to be restacked to allow even weight distribution through the whole of the rider's trunk, and the horse must be realigned, before turning is attempted again. Then correct turning and weight aids, in the direction of the movement, may be applied.

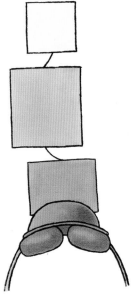

Here the rider's ribcage has shifted laterally to the left. Her weight, due to the position of the ribcage, is now loaded left – opposite to the way she wishes to travel. It is harder for her to turn her upper body in the direction of movement and she also has difficulty using her inside (right) leg properly to bend the horse, because the shift has tightened the leg from the hip.

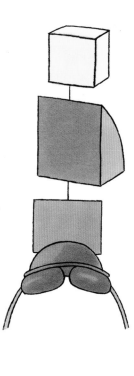

The rider is now showing much better stacking of the ribs – she is not applying an incorrect weight aid, and is able to turn her body and use her inside leg to create a better bend.

The Spine Twist exercise is key to achieving proper rotational ability when riding (see Chapter 9 Pilates Workout Exercise List). Practising the Spine Twist on the lunge will help you to become aware of how it feels to rotate the ribcage box correctly while keeping the pelvic box square and balanced.

Rib Slide exercise

This will help you to become aware of what a lateral shift of the ribcage feels like. You may like to try it in front of a mirror to check your headlights!

1. Stand with your feet about hip-width apart (you can do this sitting, too) and soften your knees a little. Place your hands on your hip bones to check for unwanted movement.

2. Keeping your headlights as level and central as possible (no tilting or twisting), try sliding your ribcage box to the left by moving your left armpit diagonally away from your right seat bone.

3. Then slide your ribcage box to the right by moving your right armpit diagonally away from your left seat bone. Which feels easier?

Starting position for the rib-slide exercise.

Sliding left.

Sliding right.

Your ribcage may tilt sideways and rotate, and possibly shift, all at the same time – the variables in the stacking patterns of all the boxes, compensatory application of aids and feedback the rider gets from the horse are infinite, since every rider feels and interprets the information differently. So, how can you monitor what the ribcage is doing? If you are thinking that this all sounds rather complex, don't worry. Actually, the solution is very simple – your elbows. Using your elbows to check the stacking of your boxes works, irrespective of the fault or combination of faults. However, despite instructions to have the 'weight in your elbows' or 'heavy elbows', or to 'BEND YOUR ELBOWS MORE!', often heard in dressage lessons, many riders struggle to find the right sensation. First, you should understand the role the elbows play in your contact with the horse's mouth, and then how they can be used to check your alignment.

Elbows and rein contact

Keeping a bend in the elbows when you ride helps you to maintain a consistent and elastic contact, and is necessary for you to communicate effective body aids, in the half-halt for example. Instability in the arm position makes these aids fuzzy and unclear. Think of your rein contact not beginning in your hands, but farther back, in your shoulders and elbows. In order to stabilise the position of the arms, and to make sure they don't get pulled straight or into 'chicken wings' (sticking out to the side), the position of other parts of the body have to be checked in a certain order. It is practically impossible to keep a bend in the elbows if your chest is depressed or tilted down at the front. So, first, make sure the ribcage and sternum are in the right place by putting the headlights on full beam. Then, squeeze the shoulder blades together to engage the trapezius, a muscle in the upper back – this stabilises the arm at the back.

This sequence shows the order in which to stabilise your arm position.

Chest is depressed, arms too straight.

Chest lifted.

Shoulder blades squeezed.

Elbows weighted and bent.

What to do to position shoulders and elbows correctly

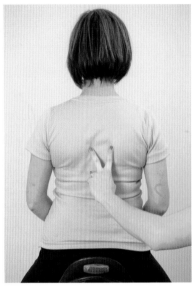

- To feel the sensation of weight in the elbows, hold your arms and hands as if you were holding the reins. Ask a friend to push lightly at the back of your elbows and resist the pressure. The upper arms must not come any farther back than vertically down from your shoulder.

- Now ask your friend to place her hands underneath your elbows and push lightly upwards. Resist downwards so your elbows drop deeper towards your hips – keep your headlights on full beam, though.

- Ask your friend to move her hands to the inside of your elbows, between your arms and waist, and to push lightly outwards, as if to send your elbows away from your body. Resist by squeezing your elbows inwards, towards your body. You should feel a sensation of heaviness or weight in your elbows and down the back of your upper arm in the tricep muscles.

Ask a friend to place her fingers between your shoulder blades and then use your muscles to squeeze her fingers closer together.

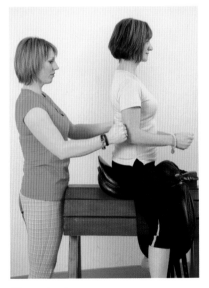

Elbows back.

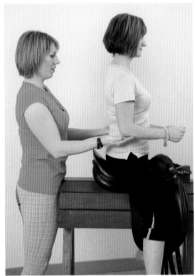

Elbows down.

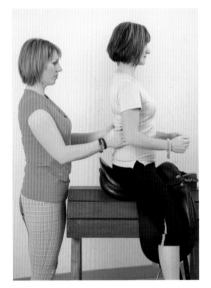

Elbows in.

While you ride, try to recreate that feeling of squeezing your elbows back, down and in to your waist. Keep your forearms soft. Being able to put a lot of weight in your elbows is sometimes called 'passive resistance' – you are not actively pulling on the horse, but through resisting in the arm, you increase the pressure he will feel if he pulls on you. It is important to release this resistance when he is working well, so you do not restrict his neck excessively. The elbows are discussed further in Chapter 7 Mysteries Unravelled – the Half-Halt.

Using your elbows as a ribcage levelling device

As long as your seat bones are reasonably level, this is a really effective way to align yourself. Bring your elbows in to your waist as described above. Now deliberately make yourself crooked – you will be able to feel, through the inside of your elbows and upper or even lower arms, that you are contacting a different part of your waist, ribcage or hips (depending on how long your upper arm is) on the lower side of your body.

Now, using your elbows, try to make contact with exactly the same part of your body on both sides.

 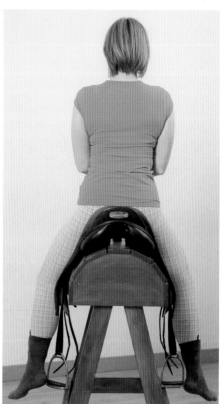

You can feel that your arms are not level when you are crooked in the saddle.

Level elbows.

Whether you have twisted, shifted, tilted, or all three, bringing your elbows in to the waist at the same point on both sides effectively stacks the ribcage centrally and squarely on top of the pelvic box. Even if you do not ride with the arms in this position throughout your session (some trainers prefer a more forward arm, although the classical dressage seat is to have the upper arm vertical), you can bring the elbows in for a few strides every so often to check yourself. It still works if you bring the elbows more to the front of your waist, as long as you contact the same point on both sides.

Look how this rider has improved her posture and helped her horse to move in a more balanced way by using her elbows to check her alignment.

The head box

At the top of the stack of boxes, the head has an important role to play. If it shifts forward, certain muscles in your neck have to work very hard to support its weight – somewhere in the region of 12lb to 14lb (5.4k to 6.4k – putting strain on the neck and shoulders. In terms of the influence on the horse, if the head box is forward of the vertical line of gravity, you are placing more weight towards the horse's forehand, which in any discipline we generally try to avoid.

If the head tilts laterally, this can be an indication of a shortening of the whole body on one side. Correcting a lateral tilt can help to align the rest of the spine – next time you ride, just glance up sharply at the peak of your hat. Is the peak parallel with the horizon, or does it tilt down slightly to one side? If it does, align the peak horizontally – a bit like a spirit level! – and feel any changes in the rest of your body.

Taking care to keep the head in neutral when riding helps to prevent the body scrunching up into crookedness. If your head is turned one way all the time, this can be an indication of a rotated ribcage.

This rider's head is pushed forwards, putting extra strain on her neck and shoulders.

By focusing on the alignment of the head box, this rider can make a huge difference to the alignment of her whole body.

Lengthening the back of the neck by visualising your neck moving towards the back of the collar while keeping the earlobes away from the tops of your shoulders and imagining cradling a peach between your chin and collar bones, can create a sense of extension and space through the entire spine.

Self-assessment

Putting the theory into practice is the next step, and a trainer with a good eye for postural imbalances is worth her weight in gold. It is fairly straightforward to make postural adjustments if you have someone constantly telling you when you have gone wrong, but if you aren't in the fortunate position of having an alignment expert watching you and a school surrounded with mirrors, which the vast majority of us aren't, ask a friend to help by watching you ride – suggest she studies the photographs and diagrams in this book, if need be. Failing that, you can make checks yourself.

Pelvic box: Can you feel your seat bones? Do they feel even, or is one more obvious than the other? If you glance down and see the zip of your breeches is not pointing vertically to the centre of the pommel, and different amounts of leather are visible in front of your thighs, your pelvic box may have slipped to one side.

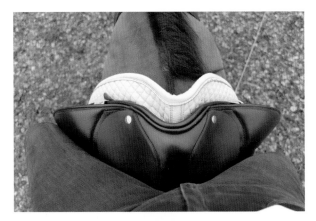

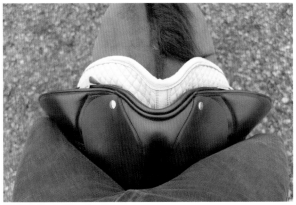

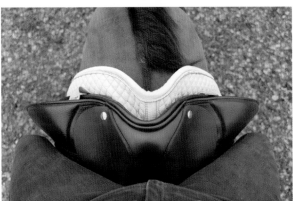

above left This rider's pelvic box has slipped.

above right This rider's pelvic box is not straight.

left A well-aligned pelvic box.

Ribcage box: If you are wearing a top with a zip or buttons, are the fasteners aligned vertically with the breeches' zip and centre of the pommel?

A ribcage stacking error – see how the zip is not vertical or aligned with the centre of the pommel.

This shows better stacking of the ribcage box.

These hand positions can indicate a ribcage stacking error.

This is better – there is equal space between each hand and the saddle, and equal distance between the withers and hands. The thumbs are up and pointing forwards to the horse's ears.

Ribcage box: Are your hands an equal distance from the withers, or are they over to one side? Is one more forward than the other? See photographs above.

Head box: Is your hat brim horizontal or on a tilt? If it is tilted, your head box is not stacked correctly on top of the other boxes.

Although it would be preferable to be totally aware of your position at all times when you are riding, and make appropriate corrections instantaneously, it is hard to think about yourself *and* ride the horse through a schooling session. Our conscious minds can cope with just a limited number of tasks at one time. For this reason, it is helpful to have specific times when you do a position check, for example, every time you pass the letter A if you are in a school, or before every transition. Eventually, it becomes a positive habit and your self-assessment will take a millisecond. Hacking is a good opportunity to concentrate on your balance and alignment while the horse is working in a constant straight line.

Useful exercises to practise on the lunge for improving balance, flexibility and alignment

Instructions appear in Chapter 9 Pilates Workout Exercise List, unless otherwise noted.

- Bow and Headlight Dazzle for establishing a level ribcage
- Sundial for rotation of the upper body
- Spine Twist for rotation of the upper body
- Cleopatra for stabilising arm position
- Thigh Drop for aligning the leg position to gravity (see page 56)
- Rib Slide for feeling how the horse follows weight (see page 46)

Sundial.

Spine Twist.

Thigh Drop exercise

This is useful for riders who struggle to get their lower legs underneath them because they sit on their bottoms too much, rather than on the correct part of the seat bones.

1. Place your hands in the prayer position and slowly curl your upper body forwards until you feel your weight drop down into your thighs, instead of remaining on your bottom. Avoid pressing your feet on to the stirrups as you do this.

2. This dropping sensation down the front of your thighs should feel a bit like kneeling. Once you have found your 'kneeling feeling', you should be able to move the lower leg back freely, without disturbing the rest of the leg.

3. Slowly uncurl your spine and return to neutral, maintaining the feeling of dropping through the thigh as you re-establish the seat-bone contact.

> ### Note
> This exercise can be done in walk on the lunge, and even off the lunge if your horse is tolerant – with your hands on the reins, obviously, and not in prayer position! – in walk and rising trot. It can take many repetitions for you to be able to maintain the length of the thigh as you return to neutral, but consistent practice does pay dividends.

The rider is not sitting on the right part of her seat bones.

Curling forward so the weight falls into the thighs.

Sitting in neutral.

The role of mechanical straightness and gymnastic straightness

As mentioned earlier in the chapter, many riders have their horses' backs treated at regular intervals, along with the six-monthly dental checks and saddle rebalances, to ensure their horses are in tip-top condition. The professionals involved offer invaluable and necessary services, but often end up making the same adjustments over and over again, because an external factor repeatedly negates the positive effects of their efforts. That factor is rider imbalance. An aware and conscientious rider will have herself treated at the same time as the horse, and so avoid placing a 'badly fitting rider' on top of a rebalanced saddle and horse. Is this enough, though?

A mechanically straightened rider, who is realigned by an osteopath or chiropractor, will probably not be aware of inherent postural imbalances, and therefore will not do the necessary strengthening work to support the therapy received. Any initial improvement will probably gradually decline as the rider continues her usual movement patterns and is drawn back into crookedness. The original muscular imbalance returns.

The gymnastically straightened rider, who may also have received chiropractic treatment or osteopathy, is aware of her postural imbalances and strives to correct them at all times. When riding, she is able to feel where the horse is crooked, because this rider starts in a neutral position and is able to prevent herself being drawn into the horse's pattern. Instead, she invites the horse to join her own straight and balanced pattern of moving. From this point, the process of gymnastically straightening the horse may begin. Both horse and rider will then require far less mechanical adjustment because gymnastic training develops correct muscle balance.

Chapter **3**

Trinity of Infinity – Breathing

Even if you follow no other instructions, learn to breathe correctly.

JOSEPH PILATES

It might seem slightly strange that so many pages are devoted to the act of breathing – after all, it's something you do all day and all night without thinking about it – but your breath and patterns of breathing can have a vast influence on your body. Your posture and alignment, levels of energy, ability to release tension and relieve discomfort are all affected by your breathing.

Relaxation exercises, yoga, tai chi and martial arts incorporate valuable breathing techniques, appropriate to each individual activity. In Pilates, 'lateral breathing', or more accurately posterio-lateral breathing, is part of the centring principle. Instead of the common pattern of airflow limited predominantly to the upper chest, or breath being directed lower into the stomach as is taught in martial arts and in relaxation techniques, breath is directed primarily towards the sides and back of the ribs during inhalation. Exhalation is supported by the conscious recruitment of the core muscles – transversus abdominus and obliques. Joseph Pilates maintained that breathing this way – with a sort of pumping action, using the lungs almost like a pair of bellows – circulates the blood effectively and awakens all the cells within the body, improving the function of every system, including the nervous, endocrine and lymphatic systems, and rids the body of fatigue-related waste products. The full inhalation and exhalation cycle is imperative during Pilates practice in order that your blood may oxygenate your muscles effectively; holding the breath at any point negates the benefit of the exercise.

In Pilates, the aim is to keep the spine, and in particular the vulnerable lower back, supported by centring the body with the activation of the deep abdominal muscle, transversus abdominus (TA). It is virtually impossible to keep the navel drawing in, and therefore the TA activated and in support of the spine, if breath is allowed to travel downwards into your stomach. Air going into the upper part of the lungs only does not oxygenate the body efficiently, because full lung capacity is not being utilised. Lateral breathing encourages a fuller breath to be taken, allowing air to travel deep into the lungs into areas not normally used, and also exhaling air from those same unused areas. This ensures that the lungs are cleared of old, stale air with each breath cycle. Consequently, I would say that lateral breathing is more energising and invigorating than it is relaxing. However, you are likely to find a release of physical and mental stress as a result of lateral breathing.

Being aware of your breathing and how changing your usual breathing patterns affects your body is important not only for good health but also for your riding. The effect of poor and good breath patterns on riding is discussed in more detail in Chapter 8 Four-dimensional Breathing.

The relationship between the flow of your breath, via the multiple muscles involved, and your psoas muscles, which operate your hips, is especially significant to riders. It's important to realise that you can direct the breath to specific areas to improve your postural alignment and reawaken parts of your body that may be so tight or inactive they are difficult to feel, contact or move. Pilates teaches you, progressively, to be more aware of your body and how it functions. The breathing exercises in this chapter work on the same basis, progressively focusing on subtle sensations.

Everybody learns at different rates and experiences the power of breath at different levels. If you find the initial exercises take a little while to master, have patience with yourself and wait until you feel confident with these before moving on to the more advanced breathing exercise. It could take days, weeks or months to reach new levels in self-awareness. Remember, it is not a race – your body will speak to you in its own time. There is little point in causing yourself unnecessary confusion and frustration by trying to notice the subtle before the more obvious is clear to you.

Breathing awareness exercise

1. Sit on a chair, or an exercise ball if you have one, facing forwards with your feet and knees about hip-width apart and your feet parallel – third toe in line with your heel. Allow the weight of your body to lean slightly to the left, so you can really feel your left seat bone.

2. Lean slightly to the right to feel the weight on your right seat bone. Do this several times, so that the contact in each seat bone is clear, before settling in the middle with your weight distributed as evenly as possible between both of your seat bones.

3. Now, lengthen your spine – imagine there is a golden thread running through your spine and out through the top of your head, and someone is gently pulling that thread towards the ceiling. Take care not to disturb the equal weighting of your seat bones as you do this. Let your eyes settle on a point in front of you and allow the muscles around your eyes to soften. You can even close your eyes if you wish, which can help you to tune in to your body's responses.

4. Wrap your arms across your chest and place your right hand on the side of your left ribcage and your left hand on the side of your right ribcage. If this is uncomfortable, place your left hand on your left ribcage and your right hand on your right ribcage.

5. Instead of allowing the air you are inhaling to settle at the front or the top of your chest, imagine your lungs are a pair of bellows and see if you can send your breath a little farther down, so that your hands become a little wider apart as you inhale. The aim is to direct breath sideways, so try to breathe 'into your hands' and really feel the contact between your inhalation and your hands on your ribcage.

Starting position for the breathing awareness exercise.

The ribs widen as you inhale.

The ribs narrow as you exhale.

> **Note**
>
> - As air is expelled, the ribcage narrows and your hands sink inwards. It is sometimes helpful to imagine that, as your lungs expand sideways and then contract, your hands are moving away from and then towards each other, as if you are playing a concertina. This motion should be smooth and flowing, not forced or harsh – keep the music playing continuously.
>
> - You can practise this breathing technique while lying on the floor, which has the advantage of providing extra feedback. As well as feeling the effect of sending the air sideways to widen the ribcage with your hands, notice how the contact between the back of your ribcage and the floor gently increases as you inhale and decreases slightly when the ribcage narrows as you exhale.

Benefits of lateral breathing

This type of breathing is used continuously during Pilates exercises, not just to help you lengthen your spine. This is done to start with to ensure that your ribcage box is not squashed down at the front or shunted backwards, and to enable you to use your lung capacity more fully. Making sure you are taking in enough oxygen for whatever you are doing means you will have more energy and greater stamina than you would otherwise have.

Keeping your ribcage box properly stacked and breathing correctly also projects a positive outlook to the people around you and increases your 'life force' energy. Think of the people you know who always seem to have a negative outlook on life, and probably make you feel rather drained after spending time with them because they have such low and negative energy levels. Notice the ribcage next time you look at one of them – if the ribcage box is not properly stacked, the energy balloons will quite literally be deflated. No one wants to be a 'flat', deflated personality. Radiate vitality, poise and positivity by keeping your spine lengthened and your ribcage in neutral, headlights beaming!

Developing lateral breathing

Balloon exercise

1. Start with the lateral-breathing exercise described above, preferably in a sitting position since this resembles your alignment on the horse more closely than lying down. Place your hands on either side of your ribcage, left hand on left

side and right hand on right side. Breathe wide and full, directing your breath sideways, like a concertina, into both hands. Repeat this a few times.

2. Imagine that inside your chest cavity you have two large long balloons (each one representing a lung). Now lighten the pressure of your left hand, or remove it completely, and see if you can direct your breath into the right side of your ribcage box, inflating the right balloon only. Feel how much air flows into your right lung and notice if the expansion of your ribcage causes your right hand to move much, or not.

3. Exhale and imagine the right balloon deflating. Repeat the breath cycle a few times, inhaling into the right side of the ribcage to inflate the right balloon, and exhaling to deflate it.

4. Now replace your left hand on your left ribcage and lighten the pressure of your right hand or remove it completely. Try inhaling and imagining the left balloon inflating as you direct your breath into the left side of your ribcage.

5. Exhale and sense the balloon deflating. Repeat this breath cycle a few times, again inflating the left balloon as you inhale and then exhaling to deflate it.

Note

- Notice how much air flows into the left side – that is how much your left hand seems to move as a result of the expansion of your ribcage as you inhale – in comparison with the right side, whether one side seems more difficult to inflate than the other and whether your ribs seem to expand more on the left or the right.

You may find your left and right side seem fairly equal in terms of how much movement there appears to be as you inflate and deflate your balloons during the above exercise. If your boxes are not stacked correctly, however, the muscular guy ropes that support the structure (the psoas) may be doing so more strongly on one side of your body than on the other. On the strongly held side, they can tend to become locked short and restrict movement – too much support, not enough freedom. Then the deep muscles within the ribcage, which are involved in the action of breathing, can become 'stuck' in such a pattern, in addition to the deep muscles of the abdominals and back, and the more superficial abdominal and back muscles. I have worked with riders who have barely any movement at all on one side of their ribcage as the muscles have stagnated in a tight, holding state. The process of awakening these muscles, enabling them to release their hold and offer more length and flexibility, starts with the breath.

Forced exhalation

Joseph Pilates taught that forced exhalation was beneficial to the body, because in order to take a full in-breath, you must first fully empty the lungs of stale air. Your abdominal muscles assist in expelling air strongly – for instance, when you cough – and a positive exhalation with active recruitment of the abdominal muscles helps to strengthen the core and increase the support offered to you by those muscles.

Try the balloon exercise again, breathing into both sides of your lungs at the same time, and also one side at a time. This time focus on the exhalation and really feel that you are squeezing every last bit of air out of your lungs – even when you think you have breathed out fully, continue to breathe out, drawing your stomach in as you do so. You will feel a squeezing, drawing-in sensation around your waist and your lower ribs. This is your oblique muscles working.

If you found when you did the balloon inflation that one side was easier to expand than the other, it may be that the muscles on that side are not offering as much postural support as on the other side. Weaker muscles on one side of your body have an effect on your ability to centre yourself correctly and stack the ribcage box above the pelvic box while riding. Revisiting the breathing exercise, concentrating on really expelling as much air as possible on the more easily expandable side, can help you to activate these muscles and strengthen them. This is a subtle and advanced breathing awareness technique, which may be applied to all the Pilates exercises in the later chapters, when you are familiar with the basic execution of them.

Chapter **4**

Trinity of Infinity – Centring

The principle of centring is essential in establishing core stability, which means the engagement and strengthening of muscles located deep within the body. Controlling these muscles – and you may not even be aware of some of them – helps to support and stabilise the trunk, and keep a correctly stacked skeleton in its proper alignment, particularly when movement is introduced. Any alignment or postural adjustments can become harder to maintain once you start to move, whether going about your daily routine or riding a horse, and concentrating on centring is a means of developing your ability to engage these deep muscles.

They are located close to the spine, offering support to the spinal column and helping to keep it upright and not wiggling around like a slinky. They are also sometimes termed antigravity or postural muscles. In contrast, muscles that are used mainly to initiate movement of the limbs, for example the bicep muscles, which flex the elbow, are often referred to as global muscles.

The main muscles involved in centring and core stablility are the pelvic-floor muscle, multifidus muscles, transversus abdominus (TA) and the internal and external obliques. Other postural muscles, the use of which will enable you to ride with greater balance and precision and clarity of communication, are discussed in Chapter 5 Functional Anatomy of the Rider.

Pelvic-floor muscle

This is the base of your support. It runs like a sling from your pubic bone to your tailbone (coccyx) and forms the floor of the abdominal cavity. This muscle performs the essential role of holding the bowel, bladder and womb in place, and helps you to control their functions. Pelvic-floor exercises that activate and strengthen the muscle fibres have long been recognised by medical professionals, physiotherapists and core stability specialists as giving many benefits, including reduced stress incontinence, e.g. when sneezing, coughing or laughing, increased faecal and bladder control, increased sexual pleasure for both sexes and reduced erectile dysfunction. Another benefit is increased support for the lumbar spine through the stabilising action of the multifidus muscles, which are engaged through the activation of the pelvic-floor muscle.

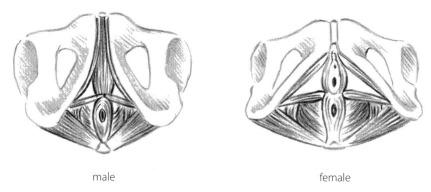

male   female

Pelvic-floor muscle.

Squeeze and lift

To activate your pelvic-floor muscle, imagine you're passing urine and you need to stop the flow. That squeezing sensation is the muscle working. Release the squeeze by imagining you are continuing to urinate. Squeeze and release a few times to sense the tightening and then the release of this muscle. Now close your eyes. Squeeze your pelvic-floor muscle to stop the flow of urine and then see if you can draw it up within your body, almost like a lift going up inside a liftshaft. Alternatively, imagine that the pelvic-floor muscle is a tissue lining the bottom of your pelvis and you are gently picking up the middle of the tissue. The action is squeeze and lift.

It is important that the muscles in your bottom are not working as you do this. The aim is to isolate the muscle activation to the pelvic floor. While the pelvic-floor muscle does include and surround the anal sphincter, any tight squeezing of the buttocks is likely to mask the squeeze and lift sensation you are focusing on. If you're not sure whether your buttocks are engaging, squeeze them as tightly as you can and then relax completely and let the cheeks go soft and floppy. Squeeze them as tightly as you can again before letting them go soft and floppy once more. Taking care to maintain the soft and floppy feel in your buttocks, try the pelvic-floor squeeze and lift again.

Multifidus muscles

While you are engaging the pelvic-floor muscle, you may feel a slight tightening or subtle pressure in your spine, if you notice any sensation there at all. Some people feel this all the way up the spine, some in the neck or below the base of the skull, some even in their ears, but if you don't feel anything, don't worry. The sensation is caused by the tightening of the tiny multifidus muscles. These run all the way up each side of the spine, from transverse to spinous process, and are important stabilisers of the spinal column. They are mostly connected to alternate vertebrae, although some of the lower ones, particularly in the lumbar spine, span more than one vertebra.

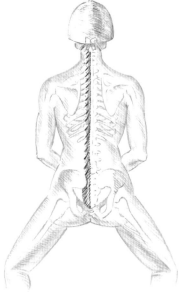

Multifidus muscles.

Support for an injured back

An impact or injury to the spine may leave some of these deep multifidus muscles in a hypotonic (not enough tone) or hypertonic (too tight) state. This can not only alter spinal alignment, but due to the changes in support offered to the spine by these stabilising muscles, it also increases the likelihood of more injuries in the future, with your back 'going' on a regular basis. The relationship of the multifidus to the pelvic-floor muscle means support can be given to a previously injured back through strengthening the pelvic floor. As most riders have had at least a few falls, probably including the odd one on the back, we would do well to make sure, in addition to all our gadgets and gizmos of back supports, body protectors and air-filled jackets, we take care of our internal structural support system.

The engagement of the multifidus enables the pelvic-floor muscle to help with balance. The role of the pelvic floor in spinal alignment and therefore balance was made very apparent to me shortly after the birth of my second child (normal delivery) when I could not step onto a wobble board at my Pilates instructor's studio. After trying several times under her watchful eye, she instructed me to activate my pelvic-floor muscle more and in particular the left side. I could feel muscle activity on the right side radiating into my inner thigh a little, but nothing much on the left at all. I practised for a week and managed to find some sensation in the left side of my pelvic floor and also in my oblique muscles, which were rather sleepy. The following week I could step on a wobble board without a problem.

Many women suffer with back pain after giving birth. The supportive muscles of the back, as well as the pelvic floor, have been overloaded and weakened, and effort and attention is required to regain tone. Unfortunately, although lip service may be paid to pelvic-floor exercises after a normal delivery, it is seldom made clear how important the strength of the pelvic floor is to spinal support.

Transversus abdominus (TA)

This muscle is probably given more attention than any other in Pilates because it is the deepest of the abdominal muscles and the one most concerned with centring the body – activating this muscle provides support for the spine. Think of it as an internal version of a back support for riders – a really wide belt that wraps around your lower back and stomach. Develop the support that your TA offers you and you should not need to purchase one of those.

Activating your TA

To feel your TA working, draw in your navel as though you are putting on a pair of last year's trousers that are just too small. Even so, try to maintain a small gap between your skin and the waistband of the trousers, drawing your navel closer to your spine.

The activation of your TA is increased even more if you think of drawing your navel in and then also scooping it up towards the base of your ribcage, or the fastener of your bra. Hold for a few seconds and then release it completely. Think of this release as a 0 per cent contraction. Now pull in your navel again as firmly

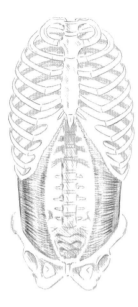

Transversus abdominus.

In this picture, the rider's TA is inactive – her fingers are in contact with her stomach.

The rider has activated her TA – look at the gap between her fingers and her stomach. She has drawn her navel in towards her spine.

as you can for a few seconds. Think of this as a 100 per cent contraction. Over time, as your TA strengthens, your 100 per cent contraction will be stronger and more supportive of your spine than it is now.

Although building up TA strength is a laudable aim, we are more concerned with stamina, and it is too difficult to maintain this 100 per cent contraction for very long without getting tense or unnecessarily tired, and you want to be able to maintain the other primary Pilates principles of breath and flowing movement. For the time being, using less effort for this exercise is a good compromise. So, draw in your navel to 100 per cent again and then release to about halfway so you are on around 50 per cent. Generally, the recommended effort level to start with is about 30 per cent, so release a tiny bit more, keeping a little gap between your stomach and the waistband of your trousers. Stick to this 30 per cent level until the principles of Pilates and the exercises are familiar. Remember, you shouldn't be tensing muscles unnecessarily (I bet you need to relax your shoulders even as you're reading this!) or holding your breath.

Just a word of caution: activating the TA compresses your abdomen and all the organs located there, so at first it is not unusual to experience the need to visit the toilet, pass wind, hear impromptu gurgling or even feel a slight stomach ache. This is quite normal, just as any muscle unused to activation lets you know of its presence when given a workout.

Internal and external obliques

The internal obliques provide support for the spine, being the next layer of muscle out from the transversus abdominus. The external obliques provide some support for the spine but are more concerned with movement. The oblique muscles, working together, can flex your spine forwards, shortening the distance between your sternum and your pubic bone. Using the obliques on one side only will flex the spine laterally, moving the ribcage box towards the pelvic box on that side to shorten the waist. The obliques on the opposite side will stretch, lengthening the waist.

Using your internal oblique on one side together with your external oblique on the opposite side will rotate your ribcage box to the side of the active internal oblique. Depending on how strongly that internal oblique is used, it may flex the spine laterally at the same time as rotating it.

The obliques are very important muscles to be aware of, particularly for riders. Injury, trauma, repetitive postural patterns and bad habits can all cause the obliques to become fixed, in which case they may continue to work to some degree even if not required. Some sections of the muscles may remain short and tight while others are longer and weaker. If the oblique muscles are not developed

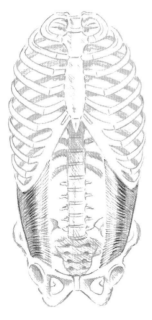

Internal obliques.

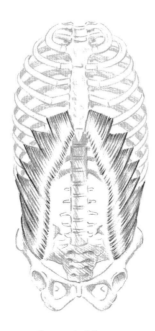

External obliques.

symmetrically and evenly on both sides, correct stacking of your boxes and your ability to turn your body with equal flexibility on both reins becomes difficult.

The activation of the obliques should always come after the engagement of the TA. It feels like an extra level of drawing in around the front, side and back of your waist, in addition to the scooping in of the navel. Most people find the obliques harder to contact immediately than the TA, and take time to learn to switch them on at will. The obliques come into action to raise abdominal pressure within the body, for instance during forced expiration when you vomit or cough. Place your fingers on your waist and cough quite loudly – you will feel the muscles go hard and then soft again. The breathing exercises and also the Pilates workout exercises will help you to find and work these muscles.

A more detailed analysis of how to apply the principle of centring to your riding is given in Chapter 5 Functional Anatomy of the Rider, and also in Chapter 7 Mysteries Unravelled – the Half-Halt.

Chapter 5

Functional Anatomy of the Rider

While you are in the saddle, your trunk is your powerhouse and centring is the principle that activates it. We have explored the action of the muscles involved, and established that achieving core stability is of paramount importance to riders, so it may seem logical to assume that the more actively centred you can be on a horse, the better your riding will be. Certainly, support for your trunk is necessary in order that you may apply hand and leg aids without compromising the balance of the seat.

However, while stability is important for resisting movements of the horse that may put you out of balance, you can have too much of a good thing. Think of stability and flexibility of the body as a sliding scale with ultimate stability – no movement – at one end and ultimate flexibility – a huge range of motion but with minimal support for joints – at the other end. Riders need to be somewhere in the middle. Too much recruitment of the stabilising muscles, by reducing the movement permitted between hips and ribcage, does not allow the necessary flexibility to absorb all the oscillations of the horse's back, and you need to do that in order to flow with the movement without blocking him. Therefore it's important to be aware of the effect that the engagement of each of the centring muscles has on you while you are in the saddle, and the subsequent effect on the horse underneath you. Used appropriately, they are helpful. Used inappropriately, they can be a hindrance. See Chapter 9 Pilates Exercise Workout List for details of the exercises mentioned in this chapter.

Pelvic-floor muscle

Although this is your base of support, it is so difficult to isolate correctly on horseback that the benefits of spinal support it offers are negated by the probable additional engagement of the buttocks and deep muscles within the hips and thighs, which should remain soft and released. Look at the diagram on page 65 to see the complexity of the muscles.

I have only ever felt it appropriate to ask pupils to engage their pelvic-floor muscles while riding in a handful of cases, and for most people it is detrimental to the maintenance of their trinity of infinity cycle.

Transversus abdominus (TA)

The TA stabilises the space between hips and ribs, reducing movement in this area, and although most of the time when riding you need to 'go with flow', there are times when stability becomes more important than flexibility – during transitions up and down, changes of rein, lateral movements, perhaps on an approach to a spooky fence, or any time the horse is being naughty and you feel insecure. During transitions, the increased force of movement on your body may cause you to lose alignment and balance. Changes of rein tend to exacerbate crookedness patterns in both horse and rider, and riders can be observed twisting their bodies into all sorts of bizarre shapes in an effort to manoeuvre the horse sideways in leg-yield, shoulder-in and half-pass.

Engaging the TA at these times can help to support the correct stacking of the ribcage and pelvic boxes until you have developed sufficient feel and balance to render the active use of it surplus to requirements. The general rule is if you don't need it, don't use it. The more correct and symmetrical the muscle balance is within your powerhouse, the less you need to use the TA, even for transitions, rein changes and lateral movements. However, you still want the TA to support your spine on a more passive basis, that is without you having to think about it and consciously activate it. Regular practice of Pilates exercises can help with this by increasing the muscle's strength and stamina.

Oblique muscles

The obliques play a huge role within the powerhouse, acting like guy ropes between your hips and ribs. If the ropes are tighter on one side than the other, along with other muscles attached to the vertebrae, the paraspinals, they will decrease the distance between the pelvic box and the ribcage box, shortening

It is a good idea to engage the TA when lifting heavy water buckets or bedding, or pushing wheelbarrows up the muckheap – using your powerhouse before and during such activities helps to reduce the strain on your spine, joints and global muscles.

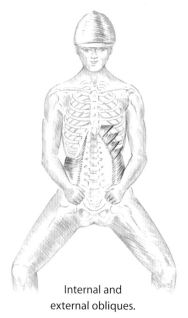

Internal and external obliques.

the waist on that side. A short waist on one side is often coupled with tight hip abductors on the same side. The hip abductors draw the leg outwards and if they are short, too, the whole of one side of you will be shorter than the other (see Chapter 10 Structuring Your Programme for instructions on how to stretch the abductors). This is often termed 'collapsed hip', which is ironic, really, since 'collapsed' implies a weakness in this area, but in fact stronger, tighter muscles are the cause of it. Muscles can only pull, not push, and the strong muscles pulling on one side make it look collapsed. Learning to engage the muscles on the opposite side, so they work harder to support you, as well as releasing tension and increasing length in short, tight muscles on your contracted side, helps counteract the problem and is necessary to develop symmetrical muscle balance in the trunk.

A dropped shoulder may also be caused by lack of symmetry in the waist area. Very often, it is not a problem in the shoulder itself, although there may be an imbalance in the muscles around the shoulder area as well. Usually, the whole ribcage is tilting downwards on one side through contracting muscles pulling it towards the pelvis.

This is another reason why, when you have established the neutral position of your pelvis, to find neutral spine you must be aware of how the ribcage box is stacked above it. Even with a correctly aligned pelvis, short muscles in the waist can pull the ribcage into misalignments, which impacts on the rein contact through compromising the symmetry of the shoulders and the elbow/hand connection. Short waist muscles may also pull the hip up, sending the weight of the pelvic box over to the opposite side.

Imbalance in the external obliques, which rotate your trunk, is another hazard. If those on one side are stronger than those on the other, your ribcage box may become fixed in mid-rotation. So instead of facing directly forwards, it will be partially turned to the left or right of the pelvic box all the time.

Driving your car, sitting in front of a computer with your legs crossed and hand forward on the mouse, and mucking out are all activities that can cause imbalance in the development of oblique muscles, with the ribcage box rotating on the pelvis or the pelvis rotating underneath the ribcage.

Contacting your obliques

Learning to contact your oblique muscles on both sides provides extra stability for the powerhouse cylinder – it is particularly helpful in reducing wobbling in all of the Pilates exercises, especially Shoulder Bridge and the side-balance exercises, such as Side Kick. Strengthening the obliques, and even consciously activating them when you are riding, helps to prevent loss of balance laterally. If you ride a very wide or round horse with little wither definition, engaging your obliques to strengthen your waist can help to prevent your saddle slipping around. Becoming aware of the longer, weaker side of your waist – the majority of people don't have equal strength on both sides – and focusing on activating the abdominals there, reduces the ability of your stronger side to pull you into misalignment, and is a powerful aid in maintaining equal weight distribution between your feet and your seat bones. Your horse will even offer a better bend by activating and shortening muscles on his long side as a result of you doing the same!

Note that pelvic rotation may be caused by a number of other factors, including muscle imbalances in the hamstrings and hip flexors and structural issues, such as scoliosis of the spine.

Remember how important the symmetrical development and strength of your oblique muscles is, both for spinal support (more the internal obliques than the externals) and the stacking of your boxes. Since they are primarily responsible for the turning of your boxes when you are riding, it is helpful to feel their action so you can notice any differences between the two sides, which would impact on your ability to ride with equal suppleness and straightness on both reins.

Obliques awareness exercise 1

When the obliques are activated on one side, they can flex and/or rotate your trunk to the same side. This exercise helps you to focus on feeling them work in that way.

1. Lie in the semi-supine position, that is on your back with knees bent and feet flat on the floor, knees and feet about hip-width apart. Pull up the pelvic-floor muscle and draw in your navel to hollow your abdominals away from the waistband of your trousers. Place your fingertips on your waist and press in gently. See photograph below.

2. Without moving any other part of your body and keeping your shoulders and buttocks soft, use just the left side of your abdomen to roll the weight of your pelvis *very slightly* to the left. Your ribcage should not roll or slide, or push over to the right, as you do this. You should feel some muscle activity underneath your left fingertips.

3. Now, use your right abdominal muscles only to return the pelvis to a central position, and then roll it *very slightly* over to the right. You should feel muscle activity underneath your right fingertips.

Feeling for the action of the obliques.

Note

- If your stomach remains hollowed throughout and you can feel your waist muscles working to achieve this small but controlled rotational movement, you are making the right connection with the obliques.

- If your stomach loses the hollowed look and feel – if you like, you can lift up your head and neck to see what's happening – you are likely to have lost both the support of the TA and connection with the obliques, and so be using other muscles.

- The movements involved are tiny, barely perceptible to an onlooker – contact with the obliques is more of an internal sensation of isolation, control and precise movement. If you can't feel the muscles becoming a little harder, like a rope tautening, use your fingertips more firmly. Sometimes added pressure can help you to feel the action, and also if the muscle isn't actually working very hard, giving your body a touch cue can wake it up a bit by opening the neuromuscular pathways from brain to body and vice versa.

Obliques awareness exercise 2

This helps you to feel the lateral flexion of internal and external obliques.

1. Lie in the semi-supine position and press your fingertips gently into your waist as in the first exercise. Make sure the pelvic-floor muscle and TA are engaged.

2. Use the right side of your abdominals to close the distance between the bottom of your right ribcage and your right hip by a *fraction* – the waist should shorten on that side. If you feel tightening in your back muscles or just underneath your armpit area, you have not made the right connection – stop and start again. Focus on achieving more of an internal sensation than a large movement, which would probably be using other muscle groups and lose the isolation of the waist. A small movement is all that is necessary. Feel how the muscle tone underneath your fingertips changes as you concentrate on drawing in the right side of the waist. The weight of your ribcage and pelvis should be equal on both sides – if you feel more weight on one side than the other and a rolling sensation as you squeeze the waist muscles, you have not isolated the obliques' lateral flexion. Stop squeezing the muscles and allow the waist to return to its resting length.

3. Try the same routine on the left side. In my experience, many people find it significantly harder to engage one side or the other, so if you don't feel much

squeeze going on, or a fluttering sensation where the muscles are switching on-off on-off, press harder and really focus all your attention on that one section of your body.

4. When you can feel each side working, try to engage both sides together to achieve that drawing in of the waist sensation.

It can take time to wake up a weak muscle or muscle group. Be patient and practise these two exercises on a regular basis, along with the Hip and Head Roll, Spine Twist and, in particular, the Side Kick. In a side-lying strength and balance exercise, the usual base of support is not available, so the body has to fire up the deep stabilisers, including the obliques, to stop you rolling over on to your back or face! The Side Kick, together with its modifications and progressions, is a good indicator of your progress in developing core-strength symmetry.

Erector spinae muscle group

This group of muscles is responsible for the extension of your spine, which, in practical terms, means it works to straighten your body after you have been in flexion. It helps to bring you fully upright after you have been bending, for instance in the Roll Down exercise; it helps you to return to a lying position after you have been sitting, for example in the Roll Up exercise; and it works to bend the spine backwards, such as in the Dart exercise. To create that feeling of length, and to create space within the body, the erector spinae group works as a team with the deep abdominals.

When you are riding, your erector spinae keep you upright and sitting tall in the saddle. When riders habitually slump and then make postural adjustments to improve their positions, the erector spinae often tire quickly because they have not been used to supporting the spine correctly. For this reason, riders who find maintaining correct length in the spine a challenge should not try to keep to a new posture throughout an entire ride but allow themselves frequent short breaks. Exercises such as Spine Stretch, Bow or Headlight Dazzle can be used to relieve the back muscles – perhaps the horse can also be allowed to stretch on a long rein.

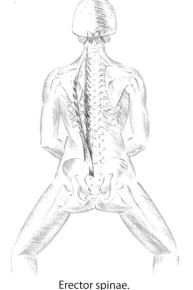
Erector spinae.

Trapezius muscle

This muscle looks a bit like a kite. Its fibres run upwards from the shoulder blades to the neck, horizontally across from the shoulder blades to the spine and diagonally from the shoulder blades all the way down to the twelfth thoracic vertebra

(T12). The engagement of the mid and lower fibres of the trapezius is necessary for stabilisation of the shoulder blades, which is important in Pilates generally because this allows the arms to work freely.

Contact with the horse's mouth does not begin in the hand or even the elbow but at the shoulder blade. Long mid-trapezius fibres, in conjunction with shortened chest muscles, contribute to a round-shouldered appearance and poor stacking of the ribcage box. Many people do not have enough scapular stabilisation and find it difficult to prevent the horse pulling them forward a little, or at least pulling their arms a little too straight, which puts a lot of strain on the neck muscles, including the upper trapezius.

Have you ever been told to shorten your reins yet again and thought, 'My arms aren't long enough to shorten them any more'? Improving the performance of your mid and lower trapezius can help to provide just enough passive resistance to the horse to prevent your body or arms being pulled out of alignment. A gentle squeezing together of the shoulder blades helps to maintain the correct stacking of the ribcage box and your headlights to stay on full beam. Excessive squeezing at an inappropriate time may result in your headlights dazzling too much, and in you holding excessive tension in the region of your lower thoracic spine. If this area feels achy, recruit the upper abdominals you use in the Bow to bring your headlights back to a level beam and practise your lateral breathing to help release tension.

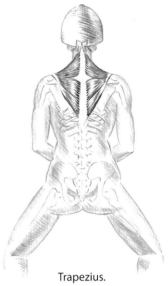

Trapezius.

Latissimus dorsi

Along with the mid and lower sections of the trapezius, the latissimus dorsi can help to stabilise your shoulder and upper arm position, allowing you to bring your arms closer to your body – particularly helpful for riders whose arms stick out like chicken wings. It assists other muscles in extending the lumbar spine, so you don't sit with your pelvic box tipped backwards, and it also helps with lateral flexion.

If you ache a bit, or feel you may be about to cramp up, in this area while practising the Pilates workout exercises, it may be that this muscle, rather than the deep abdominals, is being used to stabilise your trunk. Hip and Head Rolls, Side Stretch and Swan are useful if you need to release tension.

If you have trouble maintaining your position, particularly in the trot or canter, gently engaging the latissimus dorsi can be helpful in keeping you upright and balanced. By working in conjunction with the trapezius, it helps you to stabilise your rein contact, while you keep your lower

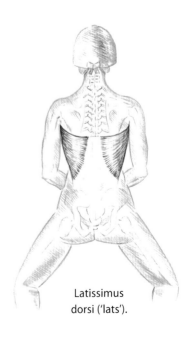

Latissimus dorsi ('lats').

abdominal region and hips soft and free to absorb the horse's motion. Excessive recruitment of the latissimus dorsi can have the same effect as excessive squeezing of the shoulder blades, and the resulting tension can be released in the same way as outlined above.

How to activate the latissimus dorsi with the spine upright

Exercises such as Dart and Swan will help to strengthen the latissimus dorsi, and being able to isolate and use them when you need to will assist in riding movements such as the half-halt. A conscious lengthening upwards and sideways of the upper fibres of your latissimus dorsi, as well as recruiting the upper abdominals, will help your alignment if you tend to have dazzling headlights and feel pressure, tension or discomfort just below your shoulder blades, or around the bra strap area of your back. Lateral breathing, and any spinal articulation exercises, such as Roll Down, Bow, Head Float (see the intermediate warm-up in Chapter 10), Roll Up and Shoulder Bridge will help with this.

As an awareness exercise, the first one below works better for me, but many clients have found they can contact their lats more easily with the second one, and also feel they can do this one when they are in the saddle. Try them both and see which one works best for you.

Latissimus dorsi awareness exercise 1

You will need a Pilates Magic Circle isotoner or, failing that, a football or anything you can squeeze between your hands – even a cushion would do.

1. Stand up and lengthen your spine. Make sure your ribcage box is not depressed – keep your headlights on full beam or you may struggle to feel the sensation of the lats activating.

2. Take your squeezable item and hold it behind you, slightly away from your bottom. Keep your arms fairly straight and your palms and fingers flat. Squeeze the object hard for about three seconds. Release. Keep squeezing and releasing for about three seconds each time. You will feel a lot of sensation in the tops and backs of your arms (triceps), and your shoulders will probably squeeze together as well.

3. Keep squeezing and releasing and now focus on the drawing-in sensation farther down, in your mid-back area. Although you will still feel the work going on in your arms and shoulders, focus your attention on the lats.

Ask a friend to place her hands either side of your spine, as shown, and imagine you are trying to squeeze them inwards. She should be able to feel the muscles moving slightly as they contract.

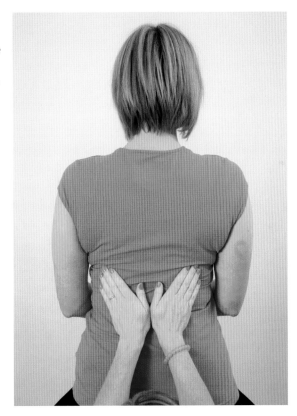

Latissimus dorsi awareness exercise 2

1. Stand straight, or sit on a chair or exercise ball. Hold your hands and arms as if you were holding the reins, with your elbows close to your waist and your fists about six inches apart, thumbs on top.

2. Start to bring your elbows into your body, but imagine somebody's hands cupping your elbows and resisting your movement as you squeeze them firmly into your waist for about three seconds. At the same time, your hands will move apart to shoulder width, fists turning upwards as they do so, thumbs pointing away from each other. Release your elbows.

3. Keep squeezing your elbows really firmly into your waist and releasing. You are looking for the same feeling of squeezing or drawing in towards the spine as in the first exercise.

Once you can contact the lats and use them to squeeze your spine, they tend to 'switch on' quite easily when you are riding, particularly in movements such as the half-halt, when your elbows would be drawn into the waist in this way anyway.

Gluteus maximus

The large and powerful gluteus maximus is a hip extensor, i.e. it opens the angle between hips and thighs, and is of huge significance to the rider because it can help you or hinder you, depending on how you use it. If the gluteus maximus muscles are engaged (even a little bit) all the time you are riding, they tend to have the effect of pulling the pelvis out of neutral into a backward tilt, sending the legs forwards. This is fine if you want the pelvis slightly tilted backwards, for instance in a half-halt, but is unhelpful for maintaining neutral as the central point of motion.

The squeezing action of the gluteus maximus encourages the backs of the thighs and inner thighs to activate, resulting in a braking effect. The horse's back muscles are prevented from transmitting the flow of energy from his hindquarters through his body. Again, this is helpful if you want to communicate a braking signal to the horse, but not if you don't. A more detailed explanation is given in Chapter 7 Mysteries Unravelled – the Half-Halt. It is often quite surprising how much even a slight engagement of the gluteus maximus – I call it a hard bottom – which you may not even be aware of, impacts on the horse's movement. I have seen hitherto lazy horses develop whole new gears when their riders take the handbrake off by releasing those cheeks and developing soft bottoms!

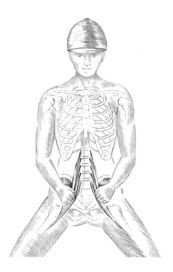

Gluteus maximus.

Psoas and iliacus.

Hip flexors (iliopsoas)

These muscles are the only ones that connect your legs to your spine. Primarily, they flex your hip joint by closing the angle between your hip and the front of your thigh, and they are so influential in your riding ability and development, a whole chapter is dedicated to a more detailed analysis of their function (see Chapter 8 Four-dimensional Breathing).

Hip lateral rotators

These muscles, located around your hip joints, rotate your thigh bone (femur) outwards and are often tight in riders. People who have a gap between their knees and the saddle, or a 'ten to two' position of the feet (are your boots always greasier on the back seam rather than the inside?) usually have particularly tight lateral rotators, this is often coupled with excessive use of the gluteus maximus (bottom constantly squeezing).

These riders benefit from regular stretching to develop a better leg position.

Notice how you stand normally – are your toes pointing outwards? if so, simply standing with your feet parallel, or with the toes pointing inwards slightly, can help to release tension in the lateral rotators. You may even feel a difference through your whole leg up to the hip by making this small change. Extreme tightness in the lateral rotators, and in particular the piriformis muscle, can be a cause of sciatica. See Chapter 10 Structuring Your Programme for a useful piriformis stretch.

Hip medial rotators

These muscles rotate the femur inwards. Slight rotation of the femur while riding is necessary to keep the knees and toes facing forwards and not sticking out away from the saddle. Riders whose legs seem to turn inwards towards one another have a slight advantage over those whose legs turn outwards, because maintaining a good leg position is more natural to them. Also, the long stirrup length necessary for dressage is easier for them to handle.

Most riders, however, tend to struggle to some degree to keep their legs in the correct position, due to tight lateral rotators. Working the medial rotators will help to stretch the laterals and allow a better leg position to be maintained. Standing with the weight evenly distributed between the feet, toes pointing in slightly, gives the medial rotators a little workout while stretching the lateral rotators.

Tight medial rotators and weak lateral rotators can also cause some discomfort in the hip area.

Hip abductors

These muscles work to bring your thigh away from the midline, shortening the distance between the outside of your thigh and your waist. While riding, both of your hip joints are abducted, since your thighs are apart in varying degrees from quite far to very far, depending on the width of the horse you are riding and the twist of your saddle. Hip abductors can often be tight because we spend so much time with the hip joints relatively fixed in the same degree of abduction.

Abductors that are shorter or stronger on one side can contract to pull the trunk over the top of the hip, causing the weight of the ribcage

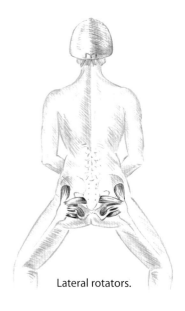

Lateral rotators.

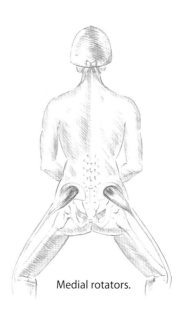

Medial rotators.

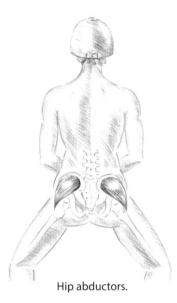

Hip abductors.

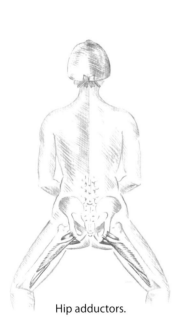

Hip adductors.

box to load the side of the tight abductors. Alternatively, they can contract to pull the thigh up towards the waist. The lack of support in the abductors on the opposite side causes the weight of the pelvic box to load the side of the weak abductors. Tight abductors can form part of the 'whole of one side shortens' alignment pattern along with the oblique and paraspinal muscles.

When using the technique that requires you to bring your legs out away from the saddle to loosen the inner thighs, it is wise to be a little cautious because when the abductors work to facilitate this movement, they can easily cramp.

Hip adductors

The adductors are located inside the thighs and are the ones working overtime in riders taught to 'grip with your knees'. You can, of course, utilise them to help you stay on board in a sticky situation, but overuse through prolonged contraction can immobilise your pelvis and lift your bottom out of the saddle. They are useful when activated in conjunction with other muscles to ride the half-halt, which is described in detail in Chapter 7, but it is important not to grip with them as a matter of course, because this can restrict your own movement as well as the motion of the horse's back. The leg-dangling exercise in Chapter 8 Four-dimensional Breathing will help to release tension held in the adductors as well as the hip flexors.

Hamstrings

Located at the back of the thighs, the hamstrings help you to apply leg aids by flexing the knee joint and therefore increasing the contact between your lower leg and the horse's sides.

There are three hamstring muscles in each of your legs – semitendinosis, semimembranosis and biceps femoris. Those nearest the midline can have a stabilising influence, with the adductors, when you use your thighs in the half-halt. An imbalance between the individual muscles in the group of three can have an influence on pelvic rotation; an imbalance between the left and right sides can be a factor in your ability to use both your legs with equal effectiveness. Someone who predominantly shows the 'whole of one side shorter' pattern (remember, an alignment pattern may well alter within a ride, depending on what the horse is doing or the movement being asked for), on the right for instance, will tend to be stronger in the right leg and hamstrings group, effectively using those muscles to hook around the horse's back and hold on, leaving the other leg flailing rather uselessly.

Pilates exercises to improve hamstring function, and therefore the speed and accuracy of the leg aids, include Single-leg Kick and Double-leg Kick. Many riders tend to be tight in the hamstrings – the shorter your stirrups, the more your hamstrings are working – and it does help to stretch these muscles. Restrictions in the hamstrings can cause problems in the lower back, and if they become so tight they are unable to release and return to a proper resting length, your ability to apply lower leg aids is compromised.

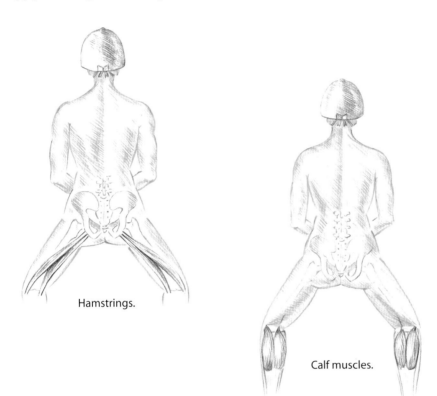

Hamstrings.

Calf muscles.

Calf muscles

The muscles of the calf are the gastrocnemius and the soleus. The gastrocnemius, along with the hamstrings, works to bend your knees, an action needed in order to apply lower leg aids, and the gastrocnemius and the soleus combine to raise the heel. The heels should be lowered in the stirrups and so any excessive contraction of the calf muscles is rather a nuisance. However, trying to force your heels down is also undesirable and can develop a lower-leg position that is way too far forward. Aside from that, it can be a tricky habit to overcome. See the photographs overleaf.

The lower leg can habitually move forward if you continually force the heel down.

Tension in the whole limb causes the lower leg to be drawn up too much.

Lengthening calf muscles and combating problem heels

A better lower-leg position can be achieved by lengthening and engaging the calf muscles. The following exercise is designed to enhance your awareness of those muscles, and can help with the problem of constantly drawn-up heels, and also heels that have been pushed too low. If you have to use a lot of lower leg, or get rub marks from your heels or spurs, try this along with the response to the leg exercise in Chapter 6 Feel, Timing and Responsiveness. In the photographs, I am giving a touch cue to the rider on her horse, but you can practise on yourself off the horse and feel the muscles working.

Calf awareness exercise

1. With your knees bent, place your fingers on the widest part of your calf and press in gently.

2. Without moving your knee, raise your heel as much as you can – really squeeze it up. You will feel the wide part of your calf becoming harder as it tightens, and you may feel also a slight upward movement – this is the muscle contracting.

The rider receives touch cues for shortening the calf muscles …

… and lengthening them.

3. Now drop your heel down as far as you can – feel the muscle lose the hardness as it lengthens.

4. Do this a few times, but instead of focusing on the heel, shift your attention to the calf muscles, concentrating on contracting or lengthening them.

If you struggle with perpetually raised heels, one way to combat it is to create a sense of weight in the leg, and lengthening your calves as you ride can help. It does take practice. A useful visualisation is to imagine your riding boots are filled with water, or made of lead, and the weight of them is drawing your lower legs towards the ground. Pilates exercises to help with this fault include Roll Down, Roll Up (legs fully extended), Spine Twist and Spine Stretch (legs fully extended).

If you suffer with the opposite problem of the heel dropping so deep that the lower leg is pushed forward and off the horse completely, try keeping a slight activation in the calf muscles as you ride – the same as you would do to draw your heel up a little – to maintain a light leg contact. Your leg will then have far less distance to travel to apply your aids. At first it can feel as though your heel is really drawn up when in fact it is still slightly below the toe, so ask someone to watch and give you feedback as the muscles get used to working a little differently. The Thigh Drop exercise can help with this fault (see Chapter 2 Trinity of Infinity – Alignment), and useful Pilates exercises include a basic Standing Position on tiptoes and Shoulder Bridge with Heel Raise.

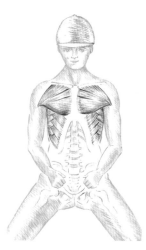

Muscles
of the chest.

Muscles of the chest

It is important not to overwork the chest muscles so much that they pull the upper arms too far forwards and inwards to give a closed appearance. This is especially likely to happen if there is also a lack of activity in the trapezius, and it contributes to a tilted-down ribcage and unstable arm position, chicken-wing elbows and probably forward head box, too. It is easier to be tipped or pulled forward with a closed chest. To keep the chest open, practise the Cleopatra and Chest Opener as well as keeping a gentle engagement of your mid and lower trapezius muscle.

'No time today'

As riders, most of us have to juggle time spent riding and with our horses with all the other aspects of our daily lives, but investing some time in your mind and body for the benefit of yourself and your horse through practising the awareness and workout exercises in this book will reap rich rewards. Even when life just takes over and you don't seem to have a minute to spare, there are still some things you can do that embody the principles of Pilates and will not disrupt your busy day. A regular routine is important to make sure that old habits do not return and new habits can be maintained and improved upon – doing a little bit, even a tiny bit, is better than doing nothing at all!

Tips to improve your spinal alignment and core-muscle stamina

- If you drive a car, next time you get in it lengthen your spine and try to find the neutral position of your pelvis and spine – weight equal through both seat bones, headlights on full beam and level. Adjust your backrest so that it neither forces you into this position nor encourages you to slump. Adjust your rearview mirror to suit the new, taller you. As you proceed on your journey, you will probably find that after a while you can no longer see in the rearview mirror quite as well because you are starting to slouch – instead of adjusting the mirror to suit your slumped spine, lengthen your spine again to suit the mirror. This starts to build stamina in the erector spinae muscles, which help you to sit tall – they can find it quite an effort to maintain correct posture and may get tired quite quickly at first, but persevere and you will soon find they can be retrained into good habits. If you get stiff after driving for long periods, try to take regular breaks and do a few Roll Downs and maybe Side Stretch exercises to keep your spine mobile and comfortable.

- When driving in a familiar area, pick out a landmark, such as a road sign, set of traffic lights or particular tree. At this point, lengthen your spine, draw your navel in towards your spine and draw in your waist muscles. Choose another landmark and see if you can keep your core connection until you reach it. If you drive this journey regularly, you can measure your progress by lengthening the distance between the landmarks each time.

- Lateral breathing can also be practised in the car – as you inhale, feel your ribs widen and sink into the backrest and then float away from it as you exhale.

- While you are making a hot drink and waiting for the kettle to boil, practise your cervical spine mobilisation exercises – head nods, tilts and turns (see Chapter 10 Structuring Your Programme). You could also practise the standing balance exercises or the standing spine and abdominal lengthening exercise, Bow and Headlight Dazzle.

- When you are sitting at your desk, or driving to and from the stables, or watching television (what do you mean no time for Pilates? Switch that television off!), practise engaging each side of your waist in turn a few times. Make sure your pelvic-floor muscle and transversus abdominus engage first. Really focus on activating the weaker side so it switches on just as easily as the strong side. Then engage both sides together for a few seconds at a time.

- Wherever you are during the day, or evening, try standing or sitting in a neutral spinal alignment and squeezing your bottom cheeks together without collapsing your chest.

Chapter **6**

Mysteries Unravelled – Feel, Timing and Responsiveness

Feel

What is feel, that mystical attribute that naturally skilled riders possess? I have heard many riding instructors say that you can't teach feel, you either have it or not, but I don't agree. Some trainers rely on that belief and as a result struggle to help riders who have positional problems that hamper the training progress of their horse. Some ignore the positional problems altogether, focusing only on the way of going of the horse, unaware that the rider's position is causing or exacerbating a training issue. Even if trainers spot problems, they often don't know enough about how the rider's body works to make improvements.

Talented and successful riders, who have no trouble with the concept of feel, often find it difficult to explain and so do not necessarily make the best teachers for those much less skilful than themselves. What they are doing may come so instinctively or habitually to them that, never having struggled with a particular aspect of riding, they can't break it down into easy steps for the less able rider to process and recreate. Their bodies work for them, not against them, as is often the case with many of us, and since they can physically interpret general concepts of riding automatically, it is hard for them to relate to someone who can't.

I think that feel can be taught, or certainly facilitated. A balanced position, effective aids, good hands and feel should not be mysteries known only to the lucky few with natural ability. Dropped shoulders, poor leg position, collapsed hips, uneven or faulty rein contact, tipping forward and leaning back, to name but a few, are all positional faults that can be corrected by identifying and working on the root cause until the rider can feel she is getting it right.

I like to think that feel is the art of conversation with your horse. The conversation works only if each party listens carefully to what the other has to say before replying or acting appropriately. If you have ever watched the very best riders in any equestrian sport, you will notice that they appear to be doing virtually nothing as they ride; the horse seems to perform of his own accord. In fact, of course, the rider's aids, instructions or directions to the horse are so subtle as to be hardly visible, because the minds and bodies of both partners are so attuned. The rider is concentrating so intently on the feedback her body is receiving from the horse that the slightest unwanted change in rhythm, balance or energy in the horse's movement is detected when it has barely occurred. The rider can sense that the horse needs a correction when the thought of losing his outline, slowing down, speeding up or spooking has scarcely formed in his mind – and a tiny error needs just a tiny correction.

This leads on to the remaining two of the big three, closely intertwined mysteries – timing and responsiveness.

Timing

The timing of your reactions and the application of your aids has a major influence on how responsive, and therefore pleasurable to ride, your horse is. To make a horse more responsive, the rider must first learn to notice potential errors very early, and become more responsive herself. Being aware of your position is a good place to start. If you know where your body should be at any point, you can start to recognise when you have moved (or been moved) from that place.

You may be thinking, 'My horse is naturally lazy/sharp/spooky/uncooperative and just won't listen to subtleties,' and it may be true that his nature is to exhibit those characteristics, but as a rider you can make him responsive. Remember, a tiny error needs a tiny correction. It is when the tiny error goes unnoticed and uncorrected that it becomes worse and worse, and then only a huge correction will work. We can all learn to ride more efficiently, so that minimum effort on the rider's part achieves maximum response from the horse. Improving your sensory awareness by learning to notice changes in how things feel will be reflected in better timing in the application of corrective aids. This ultimately leads to riding with less strength, and more technique.

Responsiveness

One aspect of riding often shrouded in mystery is the half-halt. Its technical execution is discussed in the next chapter; here we are concerned with responsiveness. The half-halt is about harnessing and modifying the horse's energy, to be directed thereafter how you choose. However, you can't harness and modify energy if there is none there in the first place – for you to be able to ride and train your horse to exhibit all the athletic qualities he displays when at liberty in the field, all his power needs to be available to you to use as you wish. This means he must be 'in front of your leg', responding honestly and with enthusiasm when you use it to ask for forward movement.

Your horse should respond instantly and continue to do whatever he has been asked to do until asked otherwise – in other words, you should not have to reapply aids to maintain an action that you asked your horse to do five minutes, or even half a circle, ago. Having to keep using your leg simply to prevent the horse from slowing down or stopping is an unnecessary waste of energy on your part, and means that he is not responding honestly to your request to go forward. This is a very common pattern in partnerships where the rider finds the horse lazy and hard work to ride.

The horse should be attuned and responsive enough to your leg so that you can ask just once for an upward transition. He should move into that pace and, without further instruction from you, maintain the same level of energy, rhythm and tempo until asked for another change. In general, the more leg that you have to use for maintenance, the less you have available to manoeuvre the horse in other ways. Also, lots of leg use makes the muscles overactive in the thighs and hips. Prolonged activity of these muscles can cause them to hold unnecessary tension, which is restrictive to the movement of the horse's back, blocking the thrusting, propulsive energy of his hindquarters – his engine. So, although you may be thinking your legs are saying 'go' or 'keep going', they may simultaneously be saying 'stop'. It is inevitable that this process becomes a vicious circle, particularly if the horse has a natural tendency to offer the bare minimum of effort.

To make sure you communicate clearly and effectively with your horse, you must mean what you say, and say what you mean; firstly, though, you need to be aware of exactly what your body is saying to the horse, so you can decide whether you mean it or not!

The role of the legs

We are often told that we must use more leg. Stronger or more frequent use of the leg will, apparently, achieve almost everything – make the horse go, make the horse stop, make him more engaged, make him rounder, make him lengthen his strides, shorten his strides, turn, bend, go sideways, stop going sideways, hold him before a jump, make him take off … the list goes on.

While use of the leg in different ways does achieve those things, in many cases when the instructor is asking you to use more leg, what you really require is more forward energy from the horse. If you can learn to use the legs in slightly different ways, depending on the response you require from the horse, it makes it much clearer to him how you wish him to react.

The following exercise is designed to help you achieve more clarity in communication with your horse, and make riding more energy efficient for you. It adheres to biomechanical principles of using your body to allow energy to flow, or the opposite. If you have free-flowing forward energy, it becomes easier to do just about everything, and especially to follow the horse's motion in a balanced and fluid way (flowing movement). Without this immediately available energy offered willingly by the horse, riding becomes rather like trying to manoeuvre a car without the engine running – very hard to steer and changing gear nigh impossible.

All the best training advice advocates the use of transitions to make your horse more responsive, and quick to move off your leg. However, it is not only the use of transitions but how they are asked for that achieves this. Riding one million transitions will do nothing whatsoever to improve the horse's way of going if they are ridden in a way that says to him, 'Hey, take your time to walk on from this halt, or trot from this walk. I'm happy to wait for you all day.' If you do what you always did, you'll get what you always got – this well-known saying is all too true in the case of transitions.

Response to the leg exercise

Remember that when you ask the horse to go forward, the muscles in your bottom and thighs must be soft and inactive. If they are switched on and hard, their squeezing action prevents your horse from moving forward freely (see Chapter 7 Mysteries Unravelled – the Half-Halt).

This exercise utilises the rule of three – ask, back up (twice if necessary), repeat. You ask the horse with a tiny aid, back up that request with a much firmer aid, then repeat your question. This is where timing becomes important. If your horse is already responsive to the leg, is too reactive or runs away from the leg, you can go straight to the response to the seat exercise, at the end of Chapter 7.

1. Apply your lower-leg aid in the way that you would really like the horse to respond to, in an ideal world – squeeze, touch, tap, wiggle, whatever suits you. For the sake of your horse, this should be a tiny, barely perceptible movement of the leg. Soft bottom and thigh muscles give his back maximum opportunity

to swing, allowing energy to flow freely through his body. If the horse does not respond by moving actively and enthusiastically forward in the pace you have in mind within no longer than two seconds, apply step two. Really movement should be instantaneous and two seconds is too long, but you can work towards that!

2. Back up your initial request with a quick firm kick to his sides with your heels. The legs must then do nothing – there should be no gripping, holding or squeezing of the horse at this point. Without actually taking your legs away from his sides, let them drop heavily towards the ground. The leg-dangling exercise in Chapter 8 Four-dimensional Breathing can help with this. It is very important that, after the sharp kick, you do not keep the leg pressure on – a holding leg is a 'containing', essentially braking, leg and we want acceleration.

By this time, the horse should have responded by moving into the pace you initially asked for with your tiny aid, maybe with a little more energy than you had planned. If so, skip to step four. If not, again within a maximum of two seconds of your second aid, move on to step three.

3. This back-up aid must be applied within a maximum of two seconds of your kick. Depending on how coordinated you are, simultaneously give the horse a quick and very firm flick with the whip (preferably on the flank, but if you prefer, on his shoulder) and also a sharp kick. If that is too tricky, just apply the whip flick.

If you have had to apply this firmer back-up aid in order to get the horse to move on from walk to trot, he must offer a bigger response than the one you initially requested. The whip or whip/kick combination should promote an instant, large and very energetic trot – the horse heaving himself reluctantly into a steady working trot is an unacceptable response. A delay of longer than two seconds, or a lack of enthusiasm in reaction, classes as no reaction at all – reapply the whip or whip/kick combination until you achieve the desired effect.

4. After allowing the horse to go forward in the new pace for a few metres, bring him back to the original pace and repeat the sequence all over again, remembering to start with the almost imperceptible aid. Continue to repeat the sequence until he responds instantly and enthusiastically to the very first tiny aid.

If the horse does not respond to that initial small request, it is imperative to continue with all the following steps of the exercise. Missing out one of them means that the learning process is compromised. It is also important that you are consistent – if you are, you will teach him to be so reactive to tiny movements it will feel like you are floating on air. If you're not, the one time you allow him to ignore your tiny aid without backing it up and making a clear correction may cause him to treat future leg requests with disdain.

So ask, back up, use a firmer back-up if necessary and repeat the sequence. We want the horse to learn to respond to that tiny aid. If you don't reapply it, you are simply teaching him that a big kick is his prompt to do whatever it is you want. If you feel no response to the tiny aid and just repeat it without applying any back-up, he doesn't know what he is supposed to do. If you ask with the tiny aid, use the back-up to elicit the response and then just carry on in the new pace, it is likely that he will forget the tiny initial aid and remember only the cruder back-up, treating this as the aid when it was in fact only a reiteration of the subtler one.

To improve responsiveness and forward energy, the horse needs to spring off very enthusiastically for a few strides only, before you bring him back to the original pace, or use the half-halt if you or he feel unbalanced. To make a horse show forward energy, it is rarely necessary to go round and round the school at high speed. Also, it is of little consequence how strong or weak your legs are – it is your leg aid that he should, and can, respond to. Ignore any instructions you may have had to 'strengthen up your legs' to make your horse more forward going – it is the intent behind the application of the aid and the timing with which the whip reinforces it, not legs of steel, that improve responsiveness.

Chapter **7**

Mysteries Unravelled – the Half-Halt

Theses and tomes written by classical riding masters advise us that the route to enlightened and exquisite riding is the perfectly timed and executed half-halt. Used to balance and rebalance the horse, it is a warning or preparatory aid, which says to the horse, 'Focus on me. I'm going to be asking you to do something in a minute.' At higher levels of training, the half-halt is used to collect the horse's steps, increase the engagement of his hindquarters and lighten his forehand.

The vast majority of riding lessons I have ever observed (and taught for that matter) have contained the instruction, 'Half-halt.' Asking the horse to perform this action is a way of checking that he is paying attention and listening to the aids.

According to the FEI definition:

The half-halt is a hardly visible, almost simultaneous co-ordinated action of the seat, the legs and the hand of the rider, with the object of increasing the attention and balance of the horse before the execution of several movements or transitions to lesser or higher paces. In shifting slightly more weight onto the horse's quarters, the engagement of the hind legs and the balance on the haunches are facilitated, for the benefit of the lightness of the forehand and the horse's balance as a whole.

Absolutely. But what exactly are the actions of the seat, legs and hands that we are supposed to coordinate?

Many trainers tell their pupils to half-halt their horses without ever telling them a) what a half-halt actually is, b) what it is supposed to achieve, c) how to do it. By that I mean precisely what they have to do with which parts of their bodies. Some may never have thought about it or been taught correctly themselves. If asked, 'How do I do a half-halt?' some look slightly quizzical as they search for a way to explain. Others give quick and confident answers, full of technical information about the finer points of the horse's balance and engagement and which hind leg needs to be in flight in order for the half-halt to be effective, but still don't tell the the rider about her own positioning, which is the information she really needs. Answers I have heard to this question include tug on the outside rein, tug on both reins, lift both reins up, lift one rein up, use your seat, hold him on your seat, brace your back, tell him to stop and go at the same time with your hands and legs, sit against him, stop following his movement, sit taller, sit deeper, sit heavier, sit lighter, resist on the reins, stiffen your body.

The interesting thing is, although some of these answers seem directly to contradict others, all of them may be appropriate, depending on the situation at the time and the individual horse and rider combination. The following sections explain exactly what to do, and why, with your legs, seat and hands to apply an effective basic half-halt, and progress to more advanced levels.

A braking aid

Whether you call the half-halt a balancing, rebalancing, preparatory, collecting, or re-energising aid, it is basically and essentially a braking aid, even if applied for just half a second to say to the horse, 'Stop what you're doing and focus on me' – a momentary pause for thought, perhaps. It is important to apply it clearly, so that you and the horse are both aware when it is on and when it is off. The two of you must understand a black-and-white language before you start communicating in shades of grey, so make sure you are both familiar with the effects of the basic half-halt before you move on to the advanced applications for subtler changes in balance and collection.

After the horse has responded to your half-halt, it is imperative that the aids are removed. You need to be aware of when the muscle power of your legs, seat and hands is on and when it is off – muscles ACTIVE and ON applies the aid; muscles PASSIVE and OFF releases it. Keeping the aids on for longer than is necessary, particularly when the desired result has already been achieved, causes the free-flowing movement of the horse to be stifled because the brakes are stuck on. It's also unnecessarily tiring for you. You have to work much harder to make a horse go when he still has the handbrake on from the last time he was stopped!

Since the aids are effective and powerful, it is sometimes better to apply them strongly for a couple of seconds, release and then reapply, and to do this repeatedly rather than holding on for a prolonged period, which could annoy or jam the horse unacceptably. I would say no longer than around three seconds is necessary for one application – if you haven't achieved your aim within that time, release the aids and reapply them straightaway along with a hand aid as a back-up. The release also offers the horse time to process and act upon your request. Horses often respond to an initial request on the release, rather than when the the aid is applied.

This is my interpretation of how to make the language of the seat accessible for riders and their horses, and it is what I have found works, both with my own horses (variety of temperaments and energy levels from the sublime to the ridiculous!) and with other partnerships. Muscles in addition to those detailed below work synergistically to assist in the actions described, but to keep things simple I think it is unnecessary to include them here. This is not meant to be an anatomical analysis of every muscle involved, as the value of that depth of technical detail for most riders is negligible, and this book is written by a rider for riders, not scientists! The activation cues below are limited to the primary muscles you need to focus on using.

Basic half-halt

For the young horse, the half-halt can be used to introduce him to the concept of seat aids. First he must be responsive to the leg aid, accept a quiet consistent contact in the mouth and know how to go, stop, and turn left and right. For the more advanced horse who already understands the seat aids, the basic half-halt can be ridden if he is being unresponsive to the subtler version for some reason.

Muscles to use

Before applying any aid whatsoever to your horse, and particularly the half-halt, lengthen your spine to ensure you don't compromise the stacking of your boxes. Do not worry that the list of things to do seems complex – work through feeling each relevant part of your body separately, then altogether, while sitting on a chair or perhaps an exercise ball. It might seem a bit mechanical at first but I assure you when you try it on your horse, it all fits together quite easily.

- Seat muscles to activate: transversus abdominus and gluteus maximus.
  How to do it: pull in your stomach and squeeze your bottom – 'hard bottom'.

- Leg muscles to activate: adductors.
  How to do it: squeeze the backs of the thighs into the saddle, keeping your lower leg slightly off the horse.

- Hand muscles to activate: trapezius, triceps and biceps.
  How to do it: squeeze your shoulder blades together, weight your elbows and squeeze your fists.

These actions should happen more or less simultaneously, but if you can activate the hands a fraction of a second after the seat and legs, so much the better.

This is a neutral seat with no excess muscle tension. The bottom and thighs are soft.

This seat shows the correct muscle engagement of the bottom and thighs for the basic half-halt.

Why does riding the half-halt in this way work?

By pulling in your stomach, you are centring your energy, supporting the spine and stabilising the section of your torso between your pelvis and your ribcage. This increased stability reduces movement in your body, which transmits to the horse as 'I'm no longer moving with your movement,' and makes it more difficult for him to swing freely underneath you. He therefore slows down to match the amount of movement you are allowing – hence a braking aid. The squeezing, almost gripping action of the backs of the thighs and the bottom act in a vice-like way on the horse's back muscles, making it very hard for him to keep the cycle of energy going from his back end to his front end since you are stopping the flow in the middle.

When you next get on your horse, practise sliding your hand under the back of your thigh and using your thigh muscles, back and front, to squeeze it – do this both sides and see if you can squeeze them equally. If one thigh seems to have less squeezing power than the other, make sure you focus on activating this side during your half-halts.

The squeezing of the shoulder blades provides further stability to the ribcage box, reducing movement between your hips and ribcage and helping to keep your headlights on full beam. The weighting of the elbows and the tightening of the fists transmit passive resistance down the rein – if he continues to propel himself forward at the same rate, the pressure of the bit in his mouth increases.

Using the muscles in this way restricts the horse's movement. Imagine how difficult it is for him to move freely forward if afterwards you forget to switch them off!

Slight backward pelvic tilt

It is helpful to visualise that imaginary bowl of water in your pelvis gently tipping back as you draw in the navel and squeeze the bottom – you do not want to drive your seat into the horse, but neither do you want your bottom to lift out of the saddle.

This picture shows a common but incorrect use of the seat – the rider has rolled right back away from neutral and is driving hard into the horse's back. This will not engage him but encourage him to drop on to the forehand as he hollows his back away from the excessive pressure.

This picture shows an incorrect use of the bottom and thighs – the seat has lifted out of the saddle because the rider is gripping too much with the entire thigh and not using abdominal tone to keep the seat bones in the saddle.

By tilting the pelvis back a tiny bit, you can ensure that the bottom of your spine lengthens down gently into the saddle, as the top of the spine lengthens upwards from the crown of your head. Your weight shifting backwards in this subtle way encourages the horse to take more weight on his hindquarters. The joint action of drawing in the stomach firmly and squeezing the bottom extends your hip joint, helping to achieve that small backward pelvic tilt. By squeezing the bottom and backs of the thighs, the front of the thighs opens slightly away from the saddle, so you don't block the horse's shoulder movement.

It is really important at this point that your ribcage box stays in place and is not drawn downwards at the front; remember that the rider's sternum dropping often results in the sternum of the horse dropping because he goes on the forehand. You need to keep thinking of lengthening upwards from the crown of your head with the headlights of your ribcage box up (the squeezing of the shoulder blades helps with this) so the whole spine does not tip on to a backward axis, putting excessive pressure on the cantle of the saddle and therefore the sensitive area of the horse's loins. Too much pressure in this area from your stack of boxes tipping back can make horses very sore in the muscles just behind the saddle. Some riders bring the spine right back in an effort to 'shift the weight back' in collection or downwards transitions, and the rider leaning back on a horse in extension is also a familiar sight. Lack of flexibility in the spine means that these riders roll way too far back to try to stay with the movement, or even drive it more.

Study magazines and you will see many riders doing this in a medium or extended trot.

Spinal articulation exercises and increasing core strength can help riders to stay in a more balanced and less invasive position.

By using the leg as described above in the half-halt and in downwards transitions, with the inner thigh muscles active but not the forward driving of the lower leg, we can differentiate much more clearly to the horse between 'going' and 'stopping' aids, in a biomechanically sensible way. Upwards transitions use the forward driving of the lower leg without the braking action of the upper leg. Lower leg for 'go', upper leg for 'whoa'. Using the leg in this way also helps the sharper horse to understand and accept the feeling of leg pressure, enabling you to use your lower leg when you need to without him overreacting to it.

More advanced half-halt

The subtler half-halt can be ridden on horses well attuned to the basic version, very sensitive horses or horses working at more advanced levels of training who need to interpret lots of variations. This type of half-halt can be used to create more collection, that is shorter, higher strides, and applied for perhaps just one of the horse's steps in any given pace; or it could be applied and released on alternate steps over a number of strides to create more expression and suspension – the momentary holding of flow within your body helps your horse to stay airborne for longer.

Muscles to use

- Seat muscles to activate: transversus abdominus, obliques, latissimus dorsi.
  How to do it: squeeze your spine.

- Leg muscles to activate: adductors.
  How to do it: close the back of the thigh, but much more gently than for the basic half-halt, almost like scooping up the horse into your body.

- Hand muscles to activate: trapezius, latissimus dorsi, tricep and bicep.
  How to do it: pull your elbows into your waist.

Why riding a half-halt in this way works

The cue to squeeze your spine relates specifically to the engagement of the latissimus dorsi, along with a low-intensity engagement of the transversus abdominus and obliques. For awareness exercises on how to contact your latissimus dorsi, see Chapter 5 Functional Anatomy of the Rider.

Engaging the lats can also be used in the basic half-halt. The difference in the more advanced version is that the strong stabilising action of the abdominals is much less, and the gripping, vice-like action of the inner thighs is negligible. The rider's movement is focused marginally more on the upper body than the lower. The lower body should be free and fluid, and able to receive and absorb the upward energy of increased collection. The pelvis stays in neutral, rather than slightly tilting, through the action of the TA and obliques.

Bringing the elbows into the waist without stiffening the forearm or wrist ensures that the resistance passed down the rein acts in more of an upward than a downward direction on the fleshy corners of the horse's mouth. This encourages a relaxing of his jaw, lifting of the head and neck and lightening of the shoulder, and therefore the increased engagement of the hindquarters. A downward/ backward action puts a lot of pressure on the very sensitive tongue and bars of his mouth.

Attune your horse to the movement of your body

For the horse who tends to work at full throttle all the time, it is helpful to teach him to be responsive to the messages transmitted by your seat and body. Then you can use your leg to direct him without him running on or running away from it, so that you don't have to hold on to his mouth all the time for brakes. Aside from that, it is useful to train any horse to be more attuned to your body and less reliant on your hand – you will eventually be able to deliver your aids so invisibly that your horse will look as though he is doing everything of his own accord.

Response to the seat exercise

The following instructions apply to the basic half-halt in sitting trot – the aids will still work in rising trot but will not be so effective. The same principles apply in canter when, depending on how powerful and strong your horse is, you will need to ride either canter-to-walk or canter-to-halt transitions.

1. Ask the horse to move forward in trot. As soon as he starts to pull a little by accelerating without being asked to, apply your half-halt body aids as firmly as you can for a couple of seconds, release and reapply as firmly as you can – this means the absolute maximum effort you can manage.

2. We want the horse to make a full transition to halt. If he doesn't halt within six seconds (again, you can work on reducing the time), make a really tight fist with your outside hand and, with a stiff elbow, give a short sharp tug on the rein. Count to six, out loud if you like. By the time you reach six you should be standing still. The horse will quickly learn that the hand aid is the back-up to the body aid – if he responds in a timely fashion to the body aid, the hand aid is either applied very gently or not at all.

3. Ask the horse to move off in trot again. As soon as he starts to lean or pull on the rein, and/or accelerate so you feel he is rushing (even a tiny bit), apply your half-halt aids with maximum effort and repeat the full transition to halt.

4. As soon as he has halted, ask him to trot once more – he must wait for your leg aid, and not move off before he is asked. If he does, apply your half-halt aids until he is immobile again.

5. This time in the trot, apply your half-halt aids as firmly as you can – either wait until he rushes and breaks tempo, or apply the aids anyway as a tester. The horse will be expecting to halt and should shorten his frame upwards and shift his weight back in preparation to stop. However, this time, instead of applying the half-halt aids for the length of time it takes for him to become immobile, as soon as you feel him begin the process of stopping, release your aids and touch him with your lower leg to send him on again in the trot. He should feel a little lighter in your hands, and a little more connected. If he has processed the half-halt correctly, he will be able to maintain balance and engagement for longer, staying softer on the reins. As soon as he does quicken, repeat the half-halt – this is literally half of a halt transition!

6. Keep repeating the body-aid half-halt, backed up with your hands if necessary every single time the horse rushes. If he starts to ignore you or take too long to respond, or you have to use your hands to keep steadying the trot, you need to go back to the trot/halt exercise to reiterate what your body aid means. If you are quick to correct him when he has just slightly accelerated, a half-halt should be all that's needed; taking longer to correct him will probably mean a full halt is necessary.

Half-halt shades of grey

The more attuned your horse becomes to the basic, black-and-white half-halt, the more you can start to ride subtler half-halts, employing shades of grey.

- Applying the same aids but for shorter periods – maybe for one of the horse's strides in any pace, or alternate strides – will have a collecting effect on his pace.

- When he understands the language of the seat, you may find that you need to activate your half-halting muscles with only half as much effort as you did when initially training him to it. Some horses require a mere suggestion of that activation. For those horses who are incredibly sensitive naturally, or become sensitive through progressive training to the centring action of the half-halt, the basic one may be too much.

- Sometimes particularly lazy horses are all too keen to reduce their level of energy input and will treat an excessively powerfully ridden half-halt as a wonderful excuse to turn the engine off completely, and you may find using the activation of the slightly different set muscles of the advanced half-halt more appropriate. Sometimes simply lengthening the spine or a deep inhalation of breath is enough.

Chapter **8**

Four-dimensional Breathing

This chapter is primarily concerned with the psoas muscles, their influence on your breath and vice versa. You have two of them, one on the left, operating your left hip, and one on the right, operating the right hip. These muscles are basically hip flexors. Since riders spend a fair amount of time with their hips in flexion, which occurs when you sit in a saddle with your feet in stirrups, most have some degree of tightness in their psoas.

The psoas muscles can help to provide stability in the lower trunk by acting as guide wires. They pass from the twelfth thoracic and the lumbar vertebrae diagonally down, out and forward, to the top of the thigh. Since they are the only muscles to attach the legs to the spine, they have a major influence on your leg position in the saddle. Depending on what position you are in, your psoas can act by moving your thigh towards your pelvis – as in moving your leg over the front of the saddle flap when you want to tighten the girth, for example, or raising your leg to place your foot in the stirrup – or by moving your pelvis towards your thigh, as in bending down to pick out hooves. Basically, these muscles close the angle between the front of the thighs and the pelvis.

Bilaterally tight psoas muscles usually mean that the angle between the hip and the thigh is stuck in a closed position, and the rider will struggle to allow the legs to drop away and hang softly in the stirrups. It is this angle that trainers seek to open with hours and hours of work without stirrups. Unfortunately, this is often off-putting for many riders, and sometimes does not reap the desired benefits anyway. A rider who is holding on to physical tension in the psoas would benefit from stretching the muscles off the horse in order to make more permanent changes to their tone and length. A rider who is holding on to mental or emotional tension in the psoas can often panic about the potential for feeling unbalanced when the security of the stirrups is taken away, thus promoting a fear stimulus if not at the precise moment the stirrups are removed, certainly at the slightest hint of excess acceleration, deceleration or lateral imbalance. This can lock the spine into a one-curve unit, causing the rider to bounce, lose balance and then feel justified in not wanting to work without stirrups! So although the psoas can serve as stabilisers, it may be better to allow them to relinquish this role due to the negative effects it can cause the rider to have on the horse's movement. If you can develop other lateral stabilisers of the seat (as detailed in the next chapter), you can allow the psoas to remain, or become, supple and free of unnecessary tension.

The breathing exercise at the end of this chapter works by encouraging more movement in your diaphragm in a flowing and unforced way, to help release excessive tension held in the psoas muscles. You may not even be aware that you were holding any tension there in the first place! The fibres of the diaphragm, especially where it attaches to the spine at the twelfth thoracic and upper lumbar vertebrae, are interwoven through connective tissue with other muscles and the psoas in particular. The twelfth thoracic vertebra (T12) – the lowest bone in your thoracic spine – is an important junction. It marks the bottom of the ribcage and, at the back, is connected to your trapezius muscle, the massive muscle that can move your shoulder blades up, together and down. At the front of T12, the diaphragm and top of the psoas muscles attach to the spine.

The location and connective tissue of the diaphragm and psoas cause the action of each to have an effect on the other. I like to think of the relationship between them as if they were holding hands. In short, stiffness and tension held in the diaphragm passes through to the psoas and vice versa. The immobilising effect of tight, short psoas on the diaphragm is a well-documented phenomenon in vocal study – singers find that they can have difficulty projecting their voices if the diaphragm is pulled downwards by tight psoas, because of the influence this has on the effective expulsion of air. Many practise Pilates and the Alexander Technique to help with the problem. Many singers also realise that the condition of the psoas/diaphragm complex has an effect on their ability to communicate emotions effectively through song.

It is important to be aware of the role of this muscle within your body, beyond its primary physical action as a hip flexor. It passes through the pelvic bowl, where some of the major organs reside, and the length and tone of the psoas influence how well those organs function. The solar plexus, an energy centre with a lot of nerve activity, is very close to the psoas/diaphragm junction and is sometimes referred to as our abdominal brain. The lumbar plexus, another bundle of nerves, passes through the psoas, and the stomach meridian in Shiatsu involves the psoas right in the belly of the muscle. It is in this area that our 'gut feelings' can be sensed. At some point you have probably ex-perienced a sudden emotion, such as shock, loss or fear, or perhaps received some terrible news, and felt almost immediately the gut-wrenching sensation in the pit of your stomach. This can be the psoas tightening in response to your emotional state.

Part of the reason why riding is so addictive and enthralling, why we want to ride in the first place, is because of the emotions that being with, and on, a horse incites within us. For some, excitement and thrills may be your motivation. For others, the fulfilling of an emotional need for love and respect – the uncondi-tional bond of closeness and communication with these beautiful creatures. Sadly, the feeling of triumph in dominating an animal drives some riders. In any case, there is no denying that riding itself is an emotive activity – the feeling of being at one (or not!) with a horse stimulates heightened states of emotion, both positive and negative. I am sure you have experienced joy, elation, pride, fear, frustration, hurt and anger while riding, as I have. These emotions affect the physical state of the psoas.

The psoas and breath

Correctly coordinating breath with movement is a major factor in making sure your Pilates practice is beneficial. Holding your breath in any way during the exercises reduces the efficiency of your body and the likelihood of develop-ing correct technique – the focus must be on making sure the breath is always flowing, and then, as you get more proficient, ensuring you work towards correct breath patterns.

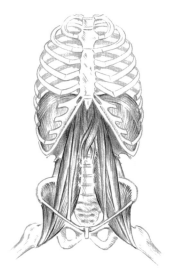

The psoas and the diaphragm.

On occasions, many riders (even when they aren't actually riding) hold their breath, or breathe in a shallow or irregular pattern. If this happens to you, it will be particularly apparent when you are concentrat-ing really hard – trying to carry out the trainer's requests when learning a new movement, for instance, or warming up before a competition, and especially as you begin your dressage test or jumping round, or if you have a hairy moment while out on a hack. Disrupted breathing inhibits the body from moving with flow because the stiffness of the diaphragm immobilises the hips through the psoas. It is also very tiring because you aren't oxygenating your muscles efficiently, which can leave you exhausted and excessively sweaty. The lack of fluidity in the hips and the tightness of the muscles restricts the horse's back muscles, preventing him from swinging and causing his strides to appear lacklustre and expressionless. His stiffening against you tends to make you work harder to regain the lost movement, and so it goes on.

If you feel that a movement or schooling session isn't really happening, try to encourage flow back into the partnership by breathing in rhythm with your horse's steps – I find that this works well even when you first get on your horse. The softer your hips are, the more he will offer you his back. In walk, try breathing in for eight steps (that is steps, not strides – eight steps is two sets of 1-2-3-4 hoofbeats) and out for eight steps. Keep this rhythm going – sharp horses may settle more quickly than they would otherwise as they tune in to the subtler communication. Lazy or tight horses can swing through more freely.

In trot, breathing in rhythm can be hugely effective in helping riders to sit better –many people feel sure that only getting ever stronger in the core will help their sitting trot, when often it is the release of the hips through breath flow that makes the difference. Breathing in for two beats and out for two beats helps to maintain swing and avoid tightening.

If it is difficult to keep this rhythm going throughout all of your school move-ments, that will help to show you where you normally start to block yourself and your horse – maybe when attempting a tricky lateral movement or transition. Lateral work is often when riders stop breathing, and wonder why the strides suddenly go 'sticky' – keep the breath flow and you may find that you discover a whole new feel. Canter works well with the breathe in for two strides, breathe out for two strides pattern.

Horses too can hold their breath if they feel tense. Bodyworker and martial artist Phil Greenfield taught me that if two people are in a room, the person with the weaker breath pattern will gradually be drawn into breathing in the same way as the person with the stronger pattern – not necessarily better, but stronger. This would explain why we sometimes feel drained of energy when with certain individuals. If your horse is tense and appears to be holding his breath, make sure you give him a good, positive and rhythmic breath pattern to follow.

The Psoas and Fear

When we are threatened by real, physical danger, certain reflex actions kick in, primal instincts geared towards helping us stay alive, and the body can react in a similar way as a result of severe emotional trauma or mentally stressful sit-uations. Fight or flight is one well-known instinct. The body is flooded with adrenaline, the heart beats faster and muscles are primed for action – in effect, we become supercharged, prepared either to stand and fight or to run for our lives. In some situations, this may be regarded as helpful. For instance, when compet-ing, a small amount of adrenaline can sharpen your reactions – being a little bit supercharged can help you to ride better. However, if the adrenaline is not used up by the physical effort engendered by your actions, your system remains flooded. The body continues to be in a state of stress, holding on to its super-charged state with heightened adrenaline levels and excess muscle tension. If the fight or flight mechanism is activated on a frequent basis but the body never fully processes the supercharge out of its system, adrenaline and tension build up more and more and a permanent state of anxiety is the result. Instead of being 'primed', your muscles end up holding on to unnecessary chronic tension and become body armoured.

Another protective reaction is the 'freeze' mechanism, or playing dead. People who are extremely frightened in a riding situation, and not just experiencing performance anxiety, may start to freeze as soon as they put a foot in the stirrup to mount. Some even find their mouths going dry and hearts beating faster, or they may feel the need to go to the toilet, as they approach the horse's stable. Due to how our subconscious mind works, the physical fear response can be triggered by just thinking about riding or handling a horse. All our flexor muscles cause the body to try to close up into a ball shape, and we go stiff, making our major organs less accessible to predator attack. When a stimulus causes our bodies to adopt the foetal position (or *want* to adopt the foetal position), it is the psoas that initiate this closing of the body into flexion.

This can be very frustrating and upsetting for riders who want to enjoy their horses but feel some sense of failure because they cannot control their fear responses. It is important to recognise that your body reacts in this way to help you – to keep you safe and out of danger. Primal instincts are so strong, so embedded in your unconscious mind, that it can be a long process to over-

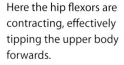

Here the hip flexors are contracting, effectively tipping the upper body forwards.

come them and move forward. It can be done, however. Working on your belief systems through techniques such as Neuro Linguistic Programming can help, although building up your skill levels through regular instruction with a trainer who knows when to support and encourage you and when to push your boundaries in a safe way is the long-term answer. If you know you can physically deal with a potential problem, it doesn't seem so horrendous. As American author J. Ruth Gendler says, 'Fear has a large shadow, but he himself is small.'

The fear reaction most often seen on horseback is the tipping forwards of the upper body, as though striving for the foetal position. Chronic muscular tension that has built up over time may be responsible for you feeling stuck in your body, physically stiff or restricted, possibly in discomfort or pain and perhaps mentally or emotionally unsettled. The body works as a whole, although many systems are working simultaneously within it. Therefore to address only the physical symptoms of tension may not be effective – we need also to work with the mind. Joseph Pilates said, 'It is the mind itself which controls the body.' Specifically in terms of the psoas – although this applies to tension being held in the shoulder area and chest, too – however diligently you practise your stretches, you will not achieve those supple following hips and pelvis and lower back, or a long, elegant and effective leg position, if the psoas are holding tension on subconscious instruction from the brain.

So how can you encourage the mind to relinquish its grasp on your hip flexors so you can get on with the business of riding? The answer is by use of the breath followed by physical release through careful stretching. Use of breath comes first because breathing really does have a huge influence on how well or not your body functions.

A different way of breathing

Four-dimensional breathing assists you to release tension, physically, mentally, emotionally and spiritually, helping you to communicate with your horse with greater sensitivity and clarity by opening the communication pathways to subtler feelings. This is a progression of the lateral breathing exercises explored in Chapter 3 Trinity of Infinity – Breathing, and is for use while riding. However, do practise off the horse first.

How to achieve four-dimensional breathing

1. Start by placing your hands each side of your ribcage. Allow the breath to flow into both hands as you inhale, feeling the ribcage expand smoothly and gently

sideways and backwards, as well as a little to the front. Try to keep your shoulders relaxed and soft – they should not rise as you breathe in. Exhale and feel your hands draw closer towards each other as the ribcage deflates. Continue to inhale and exhale, feeling the ribcage opening and closing sideways, almost like a pair of bellows. Do not push or force the ribcage outwards, or breathe any stronger than normal. You can, however, take longer breaths. Three or four seconds is a useful length of time for your in-breath, and the same for the out-breath. Notice if you seem to find it easier to inhale or exhale smoothly and evenly. Try to maintain an even flow – no big sniffs and then finding you have filled your lungs in one second! Also, be aware that to take in a full breath, it is important to have emptied the lungs as much as possible with a full out-breath beforehand.

2. The air should *flow* into your hands where they contact the ribcage, rather than be *pushed* with force. When you can feel this clearly, move your hands a little lower, on to your waist. Press your hands gently into your body – giving yourself a slightly firmer touch cue helps you to make a better mind-body connection. Continue to breathe in the same pattern. Again, do not increase the strength of breath, i.e. how much effort you are making to draw in air – no deep sniffing required – but keep the length of breath (how many seconds you are taking to inhale and exhale) the same.

Even though you have moved your hands to a lower position, still visualise directing your breath into them at the point at which they contact your body. Without actively pushing out against your hands, allow the breath to flow farther down to fill the hands in this lower position, and feel the waist smoothly widen as you breathe in and narrow as you exhale. You may like to close your eyes to assist in allowing the breath to reach lower – remember, it is a flowing, allowing sensation, not a forced, pushing action. The air will naturally flow towards the touch cue (your hands) if you give it a little time – we want the air to find the hands wherever they are placed on your trunk. Some people sense this straightaway, but for others it takes time to feel. The most important thing to remember is to quieten your mind and wait – if you allow yourself to become frustrated because your body doesn't seem to be responding, the chatter of the mind will block out any subtle changes in sensation.

3. Once you are confident that you can direct your breath towards your hands when they are placed on the sides of your ribcage and also lower down on your waist, you are ready to move on to the third position. Place your hands on the tops of your thighs, where the front of your legs meets the pelvis. Now visualise the in-breath flowing down even lower than before, through the pelvic bowl and into your hands. Exhale and feel the hands sink a tiny amount into your body. Repeat this for ten breath cycles (a complete cycle is an inhale and an exhale) and after this time notice if you feel any small change in your body. The release sensation we are looking for is subtle. People using this breathing exercise for psoas release have mentioned that:

- their hips feel softer

- they feel they are sitting deeper in the saddle and their thighs are more relaxed

- their backs feel more relaxed and they can feel their seat bones more definitely as they are 'plugged' in to the saddle.

Some have reported feeling a little light-headed, which I find interesting because it shows that their usual breath pattern does not allow as much air into the body.

Release through gravity exercise (leg dangling)

This simple but effective exercise was given to me by Phil Greenfield when I first discovered how my own psoas were affecting my body, and vice versa. It may seem as though nothing is happening but the biggest shifts sometimes happen through the subtlest changes. If you do this every day for a week, then every other day for ten days, you will allow sufficient time for gravity to assist in releasing the psoas. It is also useful for you to feel the earthing sensation of weight in the leg, which you can take forward on to your horse.

1. Stand sideways on the bottom step of a flight of stairs. Hold the banister rail with your left hand and, keeping your left foot where it is, dangle your right leg off the edge of the step so that it is floating in midair. Allow it to be free of tension and really feel the sensation of weight and heaviness in your leg – imagine you're wearing a boot made of lead, which is drawing your leg down to the floor. Feel the weight and heaviness in the leg while you breathe into the sides of the ribcage, then lower down into the back of your waist, then lower into the pelvic bowl. There is no need to sway, circle or move the leg in any way at all – simply allow it to hang there for the bones to feel 'earthed'.

2. After two minutes or so, swap legs. You will need to turn around and place your right hand on the rail, stand on the right leg and allow the left leg to dangle for around two minutes, practising your four-dimensional breathing and bringing your awareness to the increasing sensation of weight in the right leg and openness in the hip socket.

Stretches

There are many different ways to stretch the hip flexors. All of them are generally variations on a theme with differing levels of support for the lower back.

Swan.

The Swan is excellent for opening the front of the body – remember that any hint of the foetal position, tipping forwards in the saddle or sitting for long periods of time, encourages the body to shorten in front and become stuck in flexion. It is also good for stretching the quads (front of thigh muscles) and hip flexors.

Building up to performing this spinal-extension exercise comfortably may take a while. An alternative stretch for the psoas is the hip-flexor stretch described in Chapter 10 Structuring Your Programme. This needs to be performed on a clean floor, or mat, possibly with cushioning and support for the knee.

Hip-flexor stretch.

Chapter 9

Pilates Workout Exercise List

The exercises included in this Pilates workout programme will help you to recognise and maintain a neutral spine, support it with the engagement of the deep abdominal muscles, and challenge this core support with progressively increasing movement. Many other Pilates exercises exist, plus infinite variations, all of which are hugely beneficial in improving body function. Those included here have been selected specifically to mobilise the spine in the different ways needed for riding while maintaining good alignment and balance. Regular practice will improve flexion, extension, lateral flexion and rotation, and will also help increase your self-awareness of how your body is positioned, and where various parts of your body are in relation to one another.

How to perform each exercise is described in detail, together with any extra points you need to be aware of in your practice. However, Pilates is very much like riding in that you really do need a knowledgeable person watching to ensure that you are interpreting instructions correctly. It is easy to think you are doing it right, and even look like you're doing it right, while missing the point of the exercise. There is no replacement for the trained eye and hands-on corrections of a qualified Pilates teacher, and I would suggest the only way to be sure you are performing the exercises properly and for maximum benefit is to have some tuition, either in a Pilates class or preferably on a one-to-one basis. You can draw a comparison between the amount of quality learning you would achieve in a group Pilates class and a group riding lesson. You may grasp the general aims of the session, but issues specific to you would probably not be addressed in any great detail.

It is often the case that if it feels too easy, you're probably not doing it right. Keep rereading the instructions for each exercise and make sure that, over time, you incorporate all of them, plus any awareness points mentioned.

The 'no pain, no gain' ethos has no place in Pilates, so do not attempt to drive your body beyond its capabilities – the mind and body should work as one, and the mind should not be battling for supremacy over the body. If you feel discomfort at any point, go back to a more basic level and make sure you are applying all the Pilates principles. Quality, not quantity, is the key. A small movement well executed is much more beneficial than a disorganised, uncontrolled one, which may even be detrimental. If discomfort continues, or the movement becomes painful, stop and leave that exercise out of your programme. In any case, any new exercises, including the ones in this book, should not be undertaken without first consulting your doctor or health-care professional.

Key to the exercises

Exercises marked with a **blue horseshoe** are basic, introductory exercises. I would recommend that, for each position, you work at this level for a minimum of five sessions before attempting to progress to the next-steps exercises. If after five sessions you feel you need longer at this level to familiarise yourself with the programme, stick with it. It is also a good idea to revisit the basic exercises even when you have progressed, to check that you are applying all the principles of Pilates as thoroughly as you can.

Exercises marked with a **green hunt cap** are your next steps. These build on the foundations you have established in the introductory exercises and add challenge in terms of core stability, flexibility, strength and mental focus. You should notice a clear improvement in how your body functions through the regular practice of introductory and next-steps exercises before introducing advanced modifications.

Exercises marked with a **pink top hat** are advanced. Please note that most are not the full, classical, mat exercises, but modifications of basic versions. If and when you do work through to this stage, still mix in basic exercises and next-steps versions for variety, and also for revision – to make sure that you have the basic movement correct. You may be able to progress to the advanced version of some exercises much sooner than others – this is quite usual.

> ### Note
> The instruction to 'float' a limb means the movement should be free of tension and appear very graceful and flowing, as though the arm or leg is filled with helium and floating effortlessly up towards the ceiling. As you return the limb to the floor, think of it as a feather floating gently and smoothly downwards.

Standing exercises

Standing Position

Several exercises begin from the Standing Position and it is important to get it right, which may take practice.

1. Stand with your feet about hip-width apart. Make sure they are parallel, with your third toe in line with your heel. Allow your weight to shift from left to right, forward and back, all the way around the feet. Notice how the weight distribution feels through the feet. Does it feel more towards the inside of your feet or towards the outside, the heels or the toes? The aim is for it to be evenly spread. Imagine your feet are like plugs, anchoring you to the earth. Points of contact are right in the centre of each heel, on the inside of the ball of each foot and on the outside of the ball of each foot.

2. Imagine there is a golden thread running through your spine and out through the crown of your head – now imagine someone gently pulling that thread up towards the ceiling as you lengthen your spine to float the ribcage gently away from the waist.

Correct stance, aligned to gravity.

Incorrect stance, with the weight shifted forward on to the front half of the feet – a common pattern with very busy people.

Roll Down ⊔

This exercise increases flexibility and articulation of the spine (each vertebral joint moving individually, rather than in sections) as well as being a useful hamstring stretch.

1. Stand as described above, and feel the heaviness of your pelvis and the sensation of weight going down through the legs into the floor.

2. Breathe in to prepare and as you exhale draw up the pelvic-floor muscle and draw in the navel towards your spine.

3. Breathe in, and as you breathe out begin to curl your chin into your chest and roll the spine down bone by bone. As you roll farther down, transfer the weight to the front half of your feet to avoid sticking your bottom out too far behind you.

4. When you get as far as is comfortable, inhale and as you exhale start to roll back up again and restack the spine, one vertebra at a time. Ensure your pelvic-floor muscle is pulled up and your navel is drawn in throughout the exercise.

Note
- The aim is to open up all the spaces between the vertebrae, so touch the floor only if the opening up of your lumbar vertebrae allows this. There is no need to struggle. Bending from the hips just to try to touch the floor does not add any benefit to the exercise. You will be able to roll farther and farther down as your flexibility increases, and you will probably find that it feels easier after three or four repetitions.

- This is a useful exercise to do any time your back feels a little tight or stiff – perhaps first thing in the morning or after you've been sitting in the car for a long time. It doesn't matter how many breaths you take to complete the roll down and restack – in fact, if you feel any tightness or restriction during the exercise, it is a good idea to pause, breathe full and wide into the back and sides of your ribs, give the tight muscles a second to release and then continue to move as you exhale.

- As you become more familiar with this exercise, you can make it even more effective in opening up your lumbar vertebrae if you can initiate the unrolling by imagining that your tailbone is drawing down to the floor behind you. This helps to ensure that the lumbar vertebrae restack in the correct order, rather than just lifting the ribcage back up in one unit.

Roll Down.

Bow/Headlight Dazzle

1. Start in the standing position. Lengthen your spine and engage the pelvic-floor muscle and TA. Bring your hands into the prayer position with your thumbs pressed into your sternum, then slide your shoulder blades gently together and downwards towards the base of your spine. Imagine that the beam of your headlights is shining straight ahead to the wall in front of you.

exercise continues ➔

2. Breathe in, and as you breathe out, curl your upper spine forwards and engage your upper abdominal muscles to draw your sternum down and back towards your scooped in navel – the beam of your headlights will move downwards towards the floor. Keep your neck lengthened and space between your chin and collarbones – enough to cradle a peach without crushing or dropping it.

3. Breathe in, and as you breathe out, restack the vertebrae in your spine and feel the upper abdominals lengthen as you return to a neutral spine. The beam from your headlights is shining straight ahead again.

4. Breathe in, and as you breathe out, start to float your sternum, raising it farther away from your navel so that the beam of the headlights moves up the wall and towards the ceiling as your back muscles extend your spine.

5. Breathe in full and wide, and as you breathe out, engage the upper abdominals and feel the back muscles lengthen to bring your sternum down to neutral and your headlights shining straight ahead.

6. Repeat this small movement a few times, bringing your awareness to the engagement of the upper abdominals and then lengthening of the back muscles as you perform the Bow, and the engagement of the back muscles and the lengthening of the abdominals as you lift the beam of your headlights.

Note

- Notice if the movement in one direction seems to be easier than the other. This is a basic awareness exercise of front to back flexibility. It can help you stack your boxes correctly while riding and can also help to develop correct muscle balance.

Starting position for Bow and Headlight Dazzle.

Bow.

Headlight Dazzle.

Side Stretch

This exercise increases flexibility in the spine. It is also useful for stretching the obliques (side waist muscles) and to some degree the latissimus dorsi and paraspinal muscles. Do it before you ride to mobilise the spine in lateral flexion, which is how your horse's spine is positioned when on circles or in lateral movements. If you spend a little longer stretching your tight side, it will help to stop you scrunching up while riding.

1. Stand with your feet about hip-width apart and parallel, third toe in line with your heel. Take care that you do not stand with your feet turned out (in the 'ten to two' position) – riders tend to do this because usually they have tight lateral rotator muscles in the hips. Standing with feet parallel will help to stretch these hip muscles. When you are familiar with the exercise, you could even take a very slight toe-in position for variation. Shift your weight left, right, forward and back to make sure it is evenly distributed between your feet.

2. Lengthen your spine, breathe in, and as you breathe out, pull up the pelvic-floor muscle and draw in the navel towards the spine.

exercise continues ➡

3. Breathe in, and as you breathe out, float your right hand out away from your side and up towards the ceiling. Keep your shoulder down and away from your ear even though the arm is elevated.

4. Breathe in, and as you do so, stretch up as much as you can to increase the distance between your right hip and your ribcage – really feel this stretched side, but keep your pelvic-floor muscle pulled up and your navel drawn in.

5. As you breathe out, slowly slide your left hand down your thigh and allow the upper body to curve over to the left. Allow your head to tilt softly to the left so that the neck vertebrae follow the curve of the spine.

6. Breathe in and feel your breath fill the stretched side of your waist – keep your pelvic-floor muscle pulled up and your navel pulled in.

7. Breathe out and bring your body back to a central position (neutral spine) and float the arm back down to your side.

8. Repeat on the other side and then twice more on each side.

Note

- Notice if you feel a difference between the two sides. If you can't stretch one side as much as the other, hold the stretch on the tight side for a little longer than on the easy side, or perhaps take an extra breath cycle while in the stretched position before returning to neutral.

- An effective visualisation is to imagine that your body is clamped between two panes of glass and the only way you can move is sideways, with no turning or twisting of the upper body or the pelvis. Make sure your pelvis stays level as though the bottom half of your body is set in concrete. The body will often try to cheat by pushing the hips out to one side, which avoids stretching the waist muscles we are trying to target.

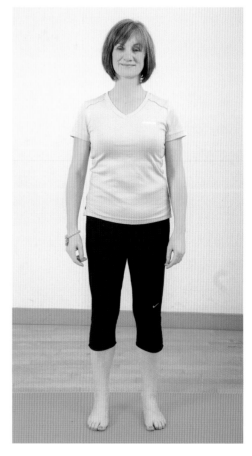

Starting position for Side Stretch.

Float your arm upwards.

Stretching the waist.

Sundial

This exercise mobilises the thoracic spine in an upper-body rotation and helps to open the chest. The isolation of movement to the upper body assists in developing your ability to turn correctly through corners, circles and lateral movements. It can also be a balance challenge since your feet – the base of your support – are placed slightly differently from the way they are positioned in the other exercises in the standing series.

1. Stand with your feet hip-width apart but with the left foot forward six inches or so. This will help to keep your pelvis still when you begin the upper-body movement.

2. Float your arms in front of you to chest height and touch your palms together. Draw your shoulder blades gently back and down.

exercise continues ➡

3. Breathe in, and as you breathe out, start to move your left hand away from your right hand, out to the side and back to the wall behind you to rotate the upper body. Follow the movement of your arm with your head – keep your gaze on your fingertips. Rotate as far as you can from your waist, keeping the pelvis still. Try to keep your weight as even as possible through both feet to ensure you aren't shifting over to one side.

4. When you have rotated as far as you can, keeping the shoulder blades drawing gently back and down, breathe in and as you breathe out, turn to move the hand smoothly back towards the other hand. Follow the hand movement with your head, keeping your gaze on your fingertips as you return to a forward-facing stance.

5. Repeat this movement three more times, and then swap feet so that your right foot is forward, and rotate to the right four times.

Starting position for Sundial.

Rotating the upper body.

Standing on One Leg

Standing balance exercises can highlight a tendency for you to take more weight through one leg than the other. Practising this simple exercise while focusing on your spinal alignment can help to educate your body to use both sides for load-bearing. Most people can quite easily stand on one leg without falling over – whether they can do it and maintain proper stacking of their boxes is another matter.

1. Start in the Standing Position, but instead of your feet being hip-width apart, move them a couple of inches closer together (only a couple). Your weight should be equally distributed between both feet.

2. Lighten the pressure going through your left foot and press down into the ground with your right foot. With the support of your pelvic-floor muscle, TA and obliques, slowly lift your left leg off the floor a few inches as you exhale – focus on maintaining absolute stability in your pelvis and ribcage, and allowing absolutely no sideways movement of your hips or ribs *at all*. You may need to practise this exercise in front of a mirror to start with.

Starting position for the Standing on One Leg Exercise.

exercise continues ➡

3. With control, lower your left foot to the floor and press down so the weight is equal again between the feet.

4. Lighten the pressure on your right foot and press down through your left. As you exhale, slowly lift the left foot, focusing on keeping your hips and ribcage level and central. Lower the foot to the floor, with control.

5. Repeat twice more with each foot, seeing if you can balance on one leg for a little longer each time.

Lifting the leg while maintaining balance.   Here the weight has shifted incorrectly.

NEXT STEPS

Standing on One Leg with Arm Float

When you can balance on one leg properly, try adding arm movement to challenge the stability in your alignment.

1. While standing on one leg, float your arms up towards the ceiling as you inhale, and back down to your sides as you exhale.

2. Alternatively, float them out to the side to shoulder height, turning your palms up towards the ceiling. Exhale as you float the arms back down, turning the palms towards your thighs.

Cleopatra

This exercise opens the front of your chest and helps to correct round shoulders, which roll forwards and inwards. Riders who struggle to maintain a bend in their elbows, or who ride with their elbows stuck out like chicken wings, will also find it very beneficial. The chicken-wing elbow can, over time, cause muscles in the upper chest to become tight, and the upper arm to be rotated inwards. This makes it easier for your horse to pull your chest box down at the front. Practising the Cleopatra exercise helps to keep your boxes stacked and your arm position more stable, even against resistance. In the suggestions for workouts (see Chapter 10), I have included this exercise in the pre-ride warm-up because it is useful to remind you to keep the feeling of weight in your elbows.

1. Start in the Standing Position, and place your arms as if you are holding a tray of drinks, with your elbows firmly against your sides, hands at waist level and your palms facing up to the ceiling, fingers flat.

2. Breathe in, and as you breathe out, start to move your hands away from each other and out to the side as far as they will go. Keep your elbows drawn in to your waist, without moving them forwards or backwards. You will feel your upper arm rotating outwards, your chest opening and your shoulder blades squeezing a little. Make sure you keep the length through your spine and particularly at the back of your neck – the head must not jut forwards.

3. Breathe in, and as you breathe out, move the hands back to the centre, keeping your elbows drawing into your waist.

4. Repeat this movement twice more and really focus on keeping the palms turned upwards, thumbs pressing towards the floor throughout.

5. This time, breathe in, and as you breathe out, move your palms outwards as before. Now breathe in, and as you breathe out, float your hands and elbows away from your body to shoulder height so you are standing in a T shape. Really lengthen your arms and reach outwards through your fingertips; press your thumbs towards the floor behind you. Making sure your sternum does not lift, slide the shoulder blades together and downwards.

6. Breathe in, and as you breathe out, draw your elbows back into your body. Breathe in, and as you breathe out, bring the hands back in front of you to the 'tray of drinks' position.

exercise continues ➡

Note

- As a variation, try this exercise with your fingers in fists, as if you were holding the reins, instead of flat.

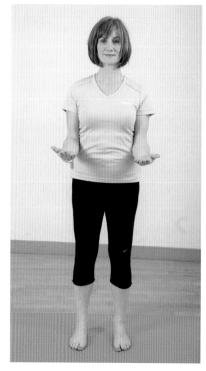

Starting position for Cleopatra.

Arms rotated.

Arms floated.

An incorrect stance with the head jutted forwards.

Semi-supine exercises

Basic semi-supine position

The semi-supine position is sometimes termed the 'constructive rest' position.

1. Lie on your back with your knees bent and your feet flat on the floor. Knees and feet should be about hip-width apart and parallel – the feet should not be turning to the inside or the outside. The weight should be completely even between your feet and plugged into the floor through the three points of contact, as in the standing stance.

2. When you first lie down on the floor in the semi-supine position, notice if you seem to have more pressure going through the left or right sides of your pelvis, or the left or right sides of your ribcage, and whether the back of your head is contacting the floor right in the centre, or slightly off to the left or right. Allow the weight of your body to sink into the floor and breathe full and wide a few times to release tension before beginning an exercise.

3. The starting point for all the semi-supine exercises is with your spine in neutral – pelvis in the neutral position and ribcage and shoulder blades stabilised. Once you can lie like this, you can challenge the stability of your trunk by adding some basic arm and leg movements. The aim is to maintain a neutral pelvis and spine through the engagement of the core muscles.

How to establish the neutral position of your pelvis

1. Create a triangle shape by placing the heels of your hands on your hip bones, your index or third fingers on your pubic bone and flattening your thumbs to your stomach – you may have to press quite hard to feel the bones – as described in Chapter 2 Trinity of Infinity – Alignment. Scoop your stomach in and tilt your pelvis back so that your lumbar spine flattens towards the floor and your pubic bone moves towards the ceiling – an imaginary glass of water positioned in the triangle would spill on to your stomach.

2. Now see if you can tilt your pelvis forward so that your lumbar spine floats right away from the floor and the hip bones move towards the ceiling – the water in your glass would spill out between your legs.

3. Repeat these movements a few times. You will feel the triangle made by your hands change its orientation – hip bones higher, or pubic bone higher. Neutral pelvis is when the hip bones and the pubic bone are on the same horizontal plane – your triangle is flat and the water in the glass is level.

exercise continues ➡

Note

- To establish a neutral side-to-side position, as well as front to back, imagine that your pelvis is like one of those old-fashioned weighing scales with two bowls, like the star sign Libra, and you have one bowl on each side of your pelvis. Make sure that each bowl contains the same weight.

- Support the neutral position of your pelvis by activating your pelvic-floor muscle and TA.

Lumbar spine flattened.

Lumbar spine raised.

Neutral spine.

How to stabilise your ribcage

Sometimes when you have moved your pelvis into neutral, you can feel an arching sensation in your back. If so, it is probably because your ribcage is not stabilised in neutral – your headlight beam is not shining vertically up to the ceiling, but is more towards your head, as in the top picture below. To lose the arching sensation, stabilise your ribcage and correctly recruit the abdominal muscles, try the following exercise.

1. Place your fingertips on your sternum and without moving your pelvis out of neutral, curl your head and neck up, as if you are going to perform a sit-up exercise.

2. As you do this, you will feel yourself rolling more on to the lower part of your ribcage and the contact between your lower ribs and the floor will increase. You will find that your sternum has moved towards your navel as the upper abdominals have engaged.

Back arched and ribcage not stablised.

Fingertips positioned so that you can feel the movement of the sternum.

exercise continues ➜

3. Slowly lower your head and neck back down to the floor, but keep the feeling of pressing your sternum towards your navel, like in the Bow exercise. This does take practice to begin with.

4. Now, without losing the neutral position of your pelvis or ribcage, gently draw your shoulder blades together and down towards the base of your spine. Recruiting the same upper abdominal muscles that you used in the Bow, keep the ribcage in neutral.

Curl up the head and neck, keeping the shoulders on the floor.

Maintain the feeling in the sternum when your head is back on the floor.

If you feel tension in your neck or have had an injury or trauma to the neck, you may find it more comfortable to use a small, firm support under your head. A folded towel no thicker than an inch is suitable.

Arm Float

1. Start in the semi-supine position. Breathe in, and as you breathe out, float your right arm up towards the ceiling and then back towards your ear. Don't take it down to the floor. Make sure your sternum does not start to lift and that you keep a drawing down sensation in your shoulder blades.

2. Breathe in, and as you breathe out, float the arm back down to your side.

3. Repeat with your left arm. Keep alternating arms – you can try breathing in, and then breathing out as you switch the arms, like a toy soldier.

4. For the Double-arm Float, inhale to prepare, exhale to float both arms up towards the ceiling and then back towards your ears. Inhale to prepare and exhale to return them to the mat.

> *Note*
> - Remember, there should be no movement of the pelvis or ribcage as you float the arms up and down.

Single-arm Float.

Double-arm Float.

Leg Slide

1. Breathe in, and as you breathe out, slide your left leg away from you along the mat, taking care to keep your pelvis and ribcage still. Draw your navel in towards your spine more and activate your obliques to minimise any movement in your trunk.

2. Breathe in, and as you breathe out, slide the leg back towards you. Repeat with your right leg and then continue to alternate legs.

3. Practise coordinating the arm float and leg slide, floating one arm and sliding the opposite leg.

Leg Slide and Single-arm Float.

Leg Float

1. This is more challenging than either Arm Float or Leg Slide. Breathe in to prepare, and as you breathe out, float your right leg up to the tabletop position – your knee bent at 90 degrees, your thigh perpendicular to the floor and your lower leg parallel to the floor, as if your lower leg is resting on a small table.

2. Breathe in, and as you breathe out, float the leg back down to the mat. The movement should be isolated to your hip socket, as though from the thigh down your bent leg is set in a plaster cast. The angle between your heel and bottom should not change at all as you float the leg up and down. Make sure your pelvis stays completely level throughout and does not roll to one side or the other.

3. Repeat with the left leg and continue to alternate legs, making sure you do an equal number of Leg Floats on each side.

Leg Float.

Leg Float with Circles

1. Float your right leg up to the tabletop position, as before. Now imagine you have a laser beam shining directly up from your knee to the ceiling. Breathe in, and as you breathe out, move your leg towards your nose, circle it across your body, then away from you, out to the side and then back to the start point. As you do this, imagine you are making a small circle on the ceiling with your laser beam!

2. Make five circles anticlockwise, then five circles clockwise before floating your leg back down to the mat. Make your circles as you breathe out, and pause after each one to breathe in. Repeat with the left leg.

> ### Note
> - The circles may be as small as an inch in diameter at first until you are able to keep the pelvis really stable while controlling the movement of the thigh bone in the hip socket. As you feel core stability improve, you can start to make the circles bigger.
>
> - Keep a weightless feeling in your leg and remember that the angle between your heel and bottom should remain the same at all times to ensure the movement is in the hip joint and not the knee.
>
> - If you get muddled with the breathing, please don't panic and start holding your breath – just *breathe*!

NEXT STEPS

Double-leg Float

This exercise reduces your base of support and so increases the challenge to your abdominal muscles. To take both legs off the mat with real control and precision requires a fair amount of core strength and stamina. Your back must be kept well supported during this exercise, and you can do this by moving the spine out of neutral and into the imprint position. This is basically a backwards tilt of the pelvis, flattening your lumbar spine towards the floor with an extra powerful engagement of the pelvic-floor muscle, TA and obliques.

1. Starting in neutral, float your right leg up to the tabletop position. Breathe in, and as you breathe out, use your abdominals to tilt your pelvis back, tipping your pubic bone up towards the ceiling.

2. Breathe in, and as you breathe out, focus on keeping the lower back glued to the floor and your abdominals glued to your spine, and float your left leg up to the tabletop position.

3. Breathe in, and as you breathe out, float your right leg back down to the mat followed by your left leg.

4. Repeat this exercise four times, alternating which leg you float up first.

> *Note*
> • Remember, if your abdominals pop up, the wrong muscles are working to stabilise you and your spine is unsupported.

Double-leg Float.

NEXT STEPS

Pelvic Roll

This exercise challenges your fine control of the obliques. Again, your back must be well supported so make sure your pelvis is in the imprint position (see above).

1. One at a time, float both of your legs up to the tabletop position. Squeeze your legs together. Move your hands a little way from your sides and turn your palms up to face the ceiling.

2. Breathe in, and as you breathe out, roll your knees a couple of inches to the left – feel the weight transfer to the left side of your pelvis.

3. Breathe in, and as you breathe out, engage your right waist muscle to pull you back to the centre.

4. Breathe in, and as you breathe out, roll your knees a couple of inches to the right, transferring the weight to the right side of your pelvis.

5. Breathe in, and as you breathe out, engage your left waist muscles to bring you back to the middle.

6. Repeat this three times each side. Make sure your pelvic floor and TA remain active so your stomach is hollow and flat throughout. Float your legs back down to the mat one at a time on an exhalation.

Ready to start with both legs in the tabletop position, but note that the palms should be facing up.

exercise continues ➡

Rolling left.

Rolling right.

ADVANCED

Toe Taps

1. One at a time, float both legs up to the tabletop, ensuring that your pelvis remains in the imprinted position (see above).

2. Breathe in, and as you breathe out, lower your right leg to tap your toe on the floor before straightaway bringing it back up to the tabletop.

3. Breathe in, and as you breathe out, lower your left leg to tap your toe on the floor before bringing it straight back up. Try to keep the same angle between your heels and your bottom throughout the exercise, so your legs are always bent at 90 degrees.

4. Toe tap each leg five times before floating your legs down to the mat one at a time on an exhalation.

> ### Note
> • Make sure your pelvis stays level and equally weighted on both sides – no rocking and rolling, tilting or shifting.
>
> • If you find your abdominals pop up or you are struggling to maintain the imprinted position, float your legs down to the mat one at a time, re-establish the correct engagement of your core muscles and try again.

Starting position for Toe Taps – both legs in tabletop.

Toe Taps are an advanced exercise, challenging for your core muscles.

Hip and Head Roll

This exercise increases rotational flexibility of the spine.

1. In the semi-supine position, bring your knees and feet together so your legs are closed. Move your arms away from your body to create a V shape on each side and turn your palms up to face the ceiling.

2. Breathe in, and as you breathe out, roll your knees to the left and your head to the right. Feel the cross stretch through your body. Make sure your pelvic-floor muscle and TA are engaged.

3. Breathe in, and as you breathe out, engage your waist muscle to squeeze your right hip a little closer to the bottom of your right ribcage and slightly backwards towards the mat. Release. Repeat this squeeze another couple of times to isolate the waist muscle.

4. Breathe in, as you breathe out, use the waist muscle to pull your pelvis all the way back to the mat – your legs will follow, rather than initiating the movement. Your head should return to the centre at the same time.

5. Repeat the whole movement, this time rolling your knees to the right and your head to the left.

Note

- Notice if there is a difference in your ability to stretch or squeeze the waist muscles on either side.

- If your oblique muscles need a little help to activate, press in with your fingertips – see the obliques awareness exercises in Chapter 5 Functional Anatomy of the Rider.

Starting position for the Hip and Head Roll exercise.

Knees left, head right.

Use your fingertips to feel the action of the obliques – and to give them a touch cue to start working.

Knees right, head left.

Pelvic tilt

1. Breathe in, and as you breathe out, use your abdominal muscles to tilt your pelvis back into the mat so your lower back flattens to the floor. Breathe in, and as you breathe out, return your pelvis to neutral.

2. Repeat the movement, and this time concentrate on squeezing your pubic bone up towards the ceiling – tilt it as high as you can by drawing up your pelvic floor and lower abdominals. Your stomach should look flat, or even hollow. If your abdominals pop up or out as you tilt the pelvis, you are using your rectus abdominus muscle (your six pack), and not the TA and obliques. Place your fingers halfway between your pubic bone and your navel to check for this as you tilt the pelvis.

3. Repeat the Pelvic Tilt and return to neutral five or six times, each time preparing to move as you inhale, and moving as you exhale.

> ### Note
> • Notice if the weight remains equal on the left and right sides of your pelvis as you tilt the pubic bone up towards the ceiling and then move back into neutral. If it rolls to one side, try to focus on distributing weight through the opposite side using your waist muscles.

Starting position for the Pelvic Tilt.

Pelvic Tilt.

Shoulder bridge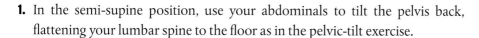

1. In the semi-supine position, use your abdominals to tilt the pelvis back, flattening your lumbar spine to the floor as in the pelvic-tilt exercise.

2. Notice that as you tilt the pubic bone towards the ceiling, your tailbone at the bottom of your spine curls away from the floor. As you inhale, imagine someone has tied a string to your tailbone; as you exhale, the string is slowly drawing up towards the ceiling and peeling your spine off the mat, bone by bone. Just peel a few bones to start with.

3. Inhale and as you exhale, start replacing the bones on the mat one by one. Your tailbone should be the last one down before you return the pelvis to neutral. Notice if one side appears to press down slightly before the other, or if the weight seems to zigzag from left to right. Concentrate on placing both sides of your back and pelvis on to the mat absolutely evenly.

4. Repeat this a few times, peeling the spine a little farther off the mat each time. Work towards being able to lift your spine up to the full Shoulder Bridge – your hips in line with your knees and your body looking like a ski slope. You can use your hands under your hips to support this position for a few seconds before returning the spine to the mat bone by bone.

> ### Note
>
> - Take care that your pelvis and hip bones remain level throughout the exercise – one side should not creep higher or lower than the other.
>
> - As you peel the spine away from the mat on the way up, and also as you replace the bones on the way down, keep the feeling of tilting the pubic bone as high as possible towards the ceiling to create a scooping sensation in the lower back.
>
> - Ensure that your neck and shoulders are as soft and free of tension as possible.
>
> - Avoid putting too much pressure on the hamstrings, which can cause cramp. Keep the weight mostly in the front half of your feet.
>
> - The knee and foot placement should not change throughout the exercise – watch out for knees rolling apart or together.

exercise continues ➔

Shoulder Bridge – peeling the spine off the mat, bone by bone.

NEXT STEPS

Shoulder Bridge with Heel Raise

1. This small extra movement tests the stability of the trunk. Start by peeling the spine from the mat as in the basic Shoulder Bridge.

2. At the top of the movement, breathe in, and as you breathe out, raise the heel of your right foot, continuing until just your tiptoes are on the ground. Make sure your left foot stays flat on the floor. As you roll up through the foot, your hip bones should be absolutely level, with no rocking, shifting or tilting of the pelvis. Any wobbling can be minimised by increasing engagement of your waist muscles.

3. Stay on tiptoe for one or two breaths and then roll back through the foot, replacing the heel on the mat on an exhalation.

4. Repeat with the left foot, keeping the right foot flat on the floor. Remember to concentrate on keeping the hips stable, and notice if it feels harder or easier to maintain your alignment on this side.

5. When both feet are flat on the floor, inhale and as you exhale, replace your spine on the mat, vertebra by vertebra.

6. Repeat the whole sequence three more times, alternating which heel you raise first each time.

Shoulder Bridge with Heel Raise.

ADVANCED

Shoulder Bridge with Leg Extension

This is a useful exercise to increase the challenge to your balance and core strength.

1. Start by peeling the spine from the mat as in the basic Shoulder Bridge.

2. Inhale and as you exhale, roll up through your right foot on to the toes and then extend your leg, keeping your knees level. Concentrate on also keeping the hips level, and the feeling of moving the sternum down towards the navel – using the same upper abdominal muscle as in the Bow.

3. If you are struggling to maintain your core stability at this point, replace the spine on the mat, bone by bone, and repeat the exercise with the other leg. If you are stable, stay up in the Shoulder Bridge and repeat the exercise with your left leg before replacing the spine on the mat.

4. Aim to extend each leg four times, peeling the spine up and rolling it down as you feel appropriate between repetitions.

Shoulder Bridge with Leg Extension.

Side-lying exercises

The side of your body is an unfamiliar base of support and side-balance exercises are effective because your core muscles have to activate quickly when you wobble to stop you rolling over! Focusing on engaging the obliques in side-lying exercises helps you to maintain correct alignment, stability and balance.

Most people find a clear difference in their ability to balance on one side compared with the other. For instance, somebody whose alignment pattern includes shorter, stronger muscles on the right side of their body usually finds it more difficult to balance when lying on their left side and vice versa. Working on being able to maintain balance and stability on the side you find most difficult can give a real sense of achievement – these exercises are a good yardstick for judging your progress in strengthening the core muscles. Progressive reduction of the base of support in the more advanced exercises increases the challenge to your core muscles. Boxes that won't seem to stay stacked properly in the saddle can be greatly assisted by the regular practice of side-balance exercises.

Starting position for side-lying exercises

1. Lie on your side with the back of your body aligned with the back of your mat (or rug or whatever you are using) and your legs extended.

2. Your joints should be stacked – that means shoulder above shoulder, hip above hip, knees and ankles together. If the exercises feel too easy, check that your hips are stacked properly. Find the knobbly lump of bone at the top of your thigh (the greater trochanter of the femur) – this is the bit you need to be balancing on. Allow your hips to roll very slightly forwards and back until you can feel this bone and find the middle of it.

3. Your underneath arm should be extended in line with your body so that the side of your head rests on your upper arm, and the palm of your hand faces the ceiling.

4. Your other hand can rest on the mat, level with your chest, fingers facing either towards your chest, directly away from your chest, or towards your head – whichever is the most comfortable for you.

5. Tilt your pelvis backwards to flatten your lumbar curve and to bring your legs forward a couple of inches, so that your body creates a shallow banana shape.

6. Flex your feet so your toes move towards your face.

7. Support this position by drawing up the pelvic-floor muscle and drawing in the navel to activate the TA. To engage the obliques, particularly on the

side resting on the floor, imagine a little mouse hole between your waist and the floor – use your waist muscle to create more space between you and the floor so that the mouse can get through the hole. Remember to increase the engagement of the oblique muscles to reduce wobbling at any point during the exercises.

Starting position for side-balance exercises.

Side Kick (levels one and two)

1. Level one – breathe in, and as you breathe out, lift your hand off the mat and smoothly place your arm down your top thigh.

2. Breathe in and as you breathe out, place your hand back on the mat. Repeat this a few times until you can perform the arm movement fluidly without any movement of the trunk.

3. Turn on to the other side of your body, align yourself in the starting position and repeat the exercise a few times. Notice if you feel any difference between this side and the other side. When you are confident you can perform this movement smoothly, move on to the next stage.

4. Level two – with your arm lying down your thigh, breathe in, and as you breathe out, raise your top leg to about hip level – keep your waist pulled up off the floor.

5. Breathe in and as you breathe out, return it to the bottom leg. Repeat this a few times keeping the trunk stable throughout. Practise this on both sides, and when you have mastered it, move on to level three.

Side-balance arm movement.

Side-balance leg movement.

Side Kick (level three)

1. With your hand on the mat, breathe in, and as you breathe out, lift both legs together off the floor, just a couple of inches. The underneath leg should lift from the hip so you feel the inner thighs working – check you are not bending your knees, and keep pushing through your heels. Hold this position for a few seconds.

2. On an out breath, lower your legs to the floor. Repeat this a few times, on both sides. When you can do it with no wobbling of the trunk, you're ready to move on to level four.

Raising both legs off the floor in Side Kick (level three).

Side Kick (level four)

1. With your hand on the mat, breathe in, and as you breathe out, lift both legs together a couple of inches off the floor.

2. Breathe in, and as you breathe out, raise the top leg to hip level or just above. Breathe in and move your top leg forward a few inches, slowly and smoothly.

3. As you breathe out, move the leg back and behind you a few inches – keep the feeling of lengthening and stretching through your leg and keep your waist pulled up off the floor.

4. Breathe in to bring the leg back to the middle and then breathe out to return it to the bottom leg. There should be no movement of the trunk at all as you kick your leg forward and back. Test the support of your core muscles by progressively making your kicking motions larger, crisper and quicker while ensuring the trunk remains stable.

> *Note*
> • As a variation, instead of kicking the leg forward and back, circle the top leg in the air, five times clockwise and five times anticlockwise. Pause between each circle to breathe in, and then circle the leg as you breathe out. Keep the circles small at first, and over time increase their size. This helps mobilise the hip joint as well as challenging the stability of the trunk.

Forward Side Kick.

Backward Side Kick.

ADVANCED

Side Plank

This is a variation of the side-bend exercise from the classical mat repertoire.

1. Lie on your side with your joints stacked and your weight resting on your underneath arm, which is bent at the elbow, palm facing the floor. Your top arm rests on your thigh. Lengthen your spine and draw your shoulder blades gently back and down. Support this position with the engagement of the pelvic-floor muscle and the TA.

2. Imagine you have a belt around your waist that is attached by a pulley to the ceiling. Breathe in, and as you breathe out, imagine your waist is being lifted towards the ceiling by the pulley to bring you into the Side Plank position. There should be as little pressure going through your forearm and legs to the floor as possible – centre all your effort into creating that lift from your waist.

3. Breathe in, and as you do so, lift your top arm off your thigh and sweep it in a graceful arc to lengthen and curve over your head, at the same time turning your head to look at the floor. Really feel the engagement of your waist muscles on the lower side as your hips lift away from the floor and you lengthen and stretch through the opposite side of your body.

Good alignment in Side Plank.

Side stretch with the arm curved overhead.

4. Breathe out to return the arm to the thigh smoothly while at the same time lowering your hips to the floor.

5. Repeat three times, then try the whole sequence on the other side. Note any differences you feel in terms of ability to use the waist muscles to lift the hips away from the floor and also how the stretch feels as the arm arcs.

Chest Opener

This is a lovely stretch to help open the chest, as well as increasing rotational flexibility in the spine.

1. Lie on your side with your legs stacked, knees bent, and your arms extended in front of you at chest level, palms touching. Breathe in, and as you breathe out, float your top arm up towards the ceiling in a smooth arc – stretch and reach through your fingertips.

2. Breathe in, and as you breathe out, smoothly float the arm back down to touch palms again. Repeat this movement twice more.

3. Next time, as you breathe out, float the arm up as before but allow your head to turn, keeping your gaze on the movement of your hand. Continue the curve of the arc a little farther, towards the floor behind you. Feel the rotation through your spine as your ribcage moves to face upwards towards the ceiling.

4. Keeping your gaze on your hand, breathe in, and as you breathe out, float the arm through the arc and down towards the bottom arm, allowing your head to roll back to its original position.

Starting position for the Chest Opener exercise.

exercise continues ➡

Vertical arm.

The full stretch.

5. Repeat this movement three more times, each time allowing your arm to continue its arc a little farther – over time, you may be able to reach the floor.

6. Repeat the whole sequence lying on your other side.

Sitting exercises

Half-seated Roll Back

1. Sit on the mat with your legs about hip-width apart and your knees bent. Your spine should be in neutral, so move around a little bit until you can feel your seat bones clearly and then make sure your weight is distributed equally between them. Sit as tall as you can to lengthen your spine and extend your arms in front of you to chest height, palms facing the floor.

2. Draw up your pelvic-floor muscle and draw in your navel towards your spine. Inhale, and as you exhale, tilt your pelvis backwards to flatten the curve of your lumbar spine – think of squeezing the pubic bone up towards the ceiling. Keep your neck long, tilting your head forward as if cradling a peach under your chin, and your shoulder tops soft and down away from your ears.

3. Breathe in, and as you breathe out, grow tall again to neutral pelvis. Repeat this pelvic tilt twice more.

4. Next time, as you exhale, tilt the pelvis back again and start to roll back a little bit farther – keep reaching through your arms and fingers – until you feel a 'biting point', where it starts to become more difficult to maintain balance. You may feel your abdominals start to judder a little. At this point, inhale, and as you exhale, grow tall from the crown of your head to restack your spine to neutral. Repeat the exercise four more times.

Note

- If your abdominals bulge out during the exercise, you are using the wrong muscles to stabilise yourself. Reduce the range of motion and ensure you can keep your abdominals hollow and scooped before attempting to roll back farther.

- Make sure that, as you roll back, the weight stays equal between the two seat bones and your body does not zigzag to left and right. Concentrate on tipping the pubic bone up towards the ceiling to open up the spaces between the lumbar vertebrae, and on squeezing your waist muscles to stabilise any wobbling.

above left Starting position for the Half-seated Roll Back.

above right Tilting the pelvis to initiate the Roll Back.

left Finding the 'bite point'.

NEXT STEPS

Half-seated Roll Back with Lobster Pincers

1. Perform the basic exercise but instead of extending the arms as before, have your elbows slightly bent and your fingertips touching at chest height, as if you are reaching around a beach ball.

2. When you have rolled back a little way, inhale, and as you exhale, open your pincers by moving your fingertips away from each other and sliding your shoulder blades together – keep the soft bend in your elbows and your neck gently lengthened and back, as though pressing into a stiff collar. Feel the extra challenge to your core stabiliser muscles with the arms open – keep your abdominals hollow and scooped.

3. Breathe in, and as you breathe out, restack your spine to neutral and close your pincers simultaneously.

NEXT STEPS

Roll Up

This exercise is excellent for improving spinal articulation – that is, the mobility between each individual vertebral joint – and is challenging to perform correctly with good abdominal connection.

1. Lie on your back with your legs hip-width apart and a small bend in your knee. Engage your pelvic-floor muscle and TA. Breathe in, and as you breathe out, float your arms up towards the ceiling and back to ear level – use your upper abdominals to keep the connection between your sternum and your navel.

2. Breathe in to float the arms up towards the ceiling, and as you breathe out, curl your chin to your chest and begin to peel the spine off the mat, bone by bone. Keeping the C shape in your spine, continue to draw the pelvic floor up and your navel into your spine until your fingers reach towards your toes. At this point, inhale and lengthen your spine into neutral, drawing the shoulder blades gently back and down.

3. Exhale to reach forwards towards your toes, tilt your chin towards your chest and use your abdominals to tilt your pelvis back, tipping your pubic bone up towards the ceiling.

4. Inhale, and as you exhale, start to unfurl your spine, using your abdominals to continue to draw the pelvis on to the mat, and replace each vertebra one by one. Squeeze your bottom and your legs together, and allow the arms to follow

the movement of the body so that by the time your head reaches the mat your arms are reaching up towards the ceiling. Float them back to ear level, your starting position, and then repeat the exercise five more times.

Unfurl the spine, bone by bone, peeling up and forwards with apparently effortless movement.

See exercise notes overleaf ➡

Note

- It is important to keep the navel scooped in and upwards to avoid the rectus abdominus or your hip flexors taking over the job of rolling you up. If your abdominals don't stay hollow and scooped throughout the exercise, work on improving this connection by practising the half-seated roll back, rolling back a little farther each time.

- You may find a point within the exercise where you feel 'stuck' – inhale and use a strong exhalation to help you engage the abdominals more deeply to move on through the exercise. If you really are stuck and cannot unfurl any farther, use your hands on your thighs to help pull you up, but progressively work on engaging the abdominals more deeply to reduce the reliance on holding your thighs.

- Maintaining flowing movement is important to avoid the exercise becoming mechanical as you roll up and unfurl. Visualise the vertebrae in your spine as a string of pearls when peeling them one by one away from the mat, and then placing them back down, smoothly and rhythmically. Try to give the illusion to anyone who may be watching that this is easy and effortless, although generally it is far from it.

ADVANCED

Roll Up with Legs Extended

1. Proceed as for the Roll Up exercise but instead of bending the knees, have your legs fully extended as you go through the movement. Squeeze your bottom and thighs together to help provide stability in your alignment.

2. Repeat the exercise six times.

Rolling up with legs extended.

> **Note**
> - If your legs want to lift away from the floor as you roll up or unfurl, push through your heels and try to increase the drawing up of the pelvic-floor muscle and abdominals just above your pubic bone to tip the pubic bone higher. Press that area with your fingers to feel where the muscles need to draw in and up.
>
> - Work on each side of your back leaving the mat at precisely the same moment, and returning at precisely the same moment. This helps to avoid any zigzagging in the movement, or your body pulling more in one direction than the other. You can deepen the engagement of your waist muscles to assist.

Basic Spine Twist

This exercise mobilises the spine in a rotating movement – the ability to rotate your upper body independently of your pelvis (and vice versa) is necessary to position your horse correctly on a circle for the lateral movements. Sometimes when instructors ask their students to turn their bodies more in the direction of the circle, the riders don't turn their bodies at all, but just their heads. The spine twist exercise helps you to learn how to rotate your upper body correctly while keeping your seat bones stable. It stretches and strengthens your oblique muscles and is a good breathing exercise because the twisting action rids the lungs of stale air.

1. Sit on the mat with your spine in neutral and your legs in prayer position – that is, in a diamond shape with the soles of the feet touching each other. If it is more comfortable, sit with your legs outstretched and your knees slightly bent, as in the half-seated roll-back exercise.

2. Find the neutral position of your pelvis – hip bones and pubic bone on a vertical plane. Rock a little bit to left and right to make sure you can feel your seat bones clearly, then keep still and make sure they are equally weighted. Lengthen your spine and support this position with the engagement of your pelvic-floor muscle and TA.

3. Place the palms of your hands together and press both thumbs into your sternum – this is the prayer position of the arms. Keep your shoulder tops down away from your ears and the shoulder blades drawn gently towards the spine.

4. Inhale, and as you exhale, slowly rotate your upper body to the left, taking care to keep your nose in line with your fingers, and your thumbs stuck to your

sternum. It is important that the weight stays equal through your seat bones as you rotate – you may be able to move just a little way at first while keeping the seat stable and your leg muscles soft. Keep as much length through the spine as possible, especially through the back of the neck, and your shoulder blades squeezing gently together and down.

5. When you have turned as far as you can, inhale, and then exhale to rotate your body back to the centre. Repeat the exercise, this time rotating to the right, and notice any difference from the previous movement. Repeat twice more each side.

Starting position for the basic Spine Twist.

Rotating to the left …

… and to the right.

Note

- It is helpful to practise this exercise in front of a mirror to check that you aren't collapsing on one side as you rotate, and that your ribcage isn't shifting sideways as you turn. Either or both of these faults are common with this exercise, and also while riding, which can give the horse a confusing weight aid. If you are riding on the right rein and intending to turn or bend your horse to the right, or position his shoulders inwards for a shoulder-in or half-pass exercise for example, your ribcage box shifting laterally to the left as you turn your shoulders to the right can encourage him to fall out through the left shoulder. The proper execution of the spine-twist exercise helps you learn to turn from the right place in your spine and will programme your body to maintain correct alignment in the saddle. *Note continues overleaf*

above left The correct starting position for the Spine Twist from the back.

above right Rotating to the right, performed correctly …

… and incorrectly.

- The same applies in reverse. If the horse has a strong tendency to fall out through one shoulder, this can encourage a lateral shift of the rider's ribcage box. Imagine the spine as a central pole going down through the ribcage and pelvic boxes. The ribcage box can spin in rotation only around the pole; it is unable to tilt or shift naturally on top of the pelvic box. As you are rotating your body to the left, try making a little lateral shift of your ribs to the left. You may have to stop halfway through rotating to do this, or even after rotating, until you are used to the movement, but work towards being able to project the ribs in the direction of movement at the same time as you rotate. When you are riding and first implement this correction, it can feel like you are leaning in when you are, in fact, correctly aligned in rotation. Make sure your weight is even on your seat bones, you are maintaining length in the spine and your elbows are pushing into your waist – if you are still unsure, ask a trainer or observer to let you know whether you appear to be leaning in or not.

ADVANCED

Full Spine Twist

1. Sit with your legs fully extended – which gives your hamstrings a stretch – and feet flexed, toes pointing towards the ceiling. Riders tend to have tight hamstrings, which can pull the lumbar curve flat when you sit with the legs extended. Therefore it is advisable to raise your bottom off the floor by sitting on a phone book or yoga block, if you have one, which will make it easier for you to maintain a neutral position of the pelvis and spine. You can also squeeze your bottom in this exercise.

2. Extend your arms out to the side at shoulder height, palms facing downwards. Breathe in, and as you breathe out, rotate from your waist, as in the basic spine twist. When you have turned as far as you can keeping your nose in line with your sternum, continue to rotate the rest of the spine right through to your head so you are looking over your shoulder. Breathe in, and as you breathe out, rotate back to the centre, head last.

Spine Stretch

This exercise, a progression of the Bow, helps to open up the spaces between the vertebrae in the upper back, and is a good breathing exercise since it opens up the back of the ribs. It is also good for releasing tension in the muscles of the back of the neck and shoulders. Include it towards the end of your workout session, particularly after such exercises as Cleopatra, Swimming, Dart, Swan and Single or Double-leg Kick.

1. Sit with your legs fully extended, if possible, feet hip-width apart and flexed. This will give you the benefit of a hamstring stretch, but if you can't manage it, have your legs in prayer position. Sit on a phone book, or something similar, if necessary. I like to have my back against a wall, because this provides valuable feedback regarding the articulation of the spine. Rest your hands between your legs and allow the crown of your head to lengthen away from the weight of your seat bones.

2. Breathe in, and as you breathe out, curl your chin towards your chest and, keeping your eyes on your navel, roll your upper spine down, bone by bone. Allow your fingers to creep forwards towards your knees like spiders, and really scoop your navel in and upwards towards the base of your ribs.

3. Breathe in full and wide to the back sides of your ribs – if you're sitting against a wall, feel the contact increase between your back and the wall. Then exhale to restack your spine, vertebra by vertebra, into neutral. Repeat this three times.

> ### Note
> - After trickling your fingers forward towards your knees, you can try creeping them over more towards one leg (increasing the hamstring stretch this side) and then creeping them over to the other leg before restacking your spine.

Starting position for the Spine Stretch.

exercise continues ➡

Peeling the spine downwards.

Creeping the fingers towards one leg.

Prone exercises

These exercises, performed while lying on your front, help to strengthen your back muscles. They also stretch the hip flexor muscles. In your Pilates workout session, it is important to include back extension exercises after you have worked the spine in neutral and flexion, to promote good front to back symmetry.

From a riding perspective, the ability to lengthen your spine and create space between your pelvic and ribcage boxes helps you take more responsibility for carrying your own weight. By strengthening your spine extensors, these exercises help to develop stamina for sitting tall, and they also help you to avoid collapsing your stomach and bracing your back inappropriately. Men may wish to place a cushion under their hips when exercising in the prone position.

Swimming

The Swimming exercise is good for developing better coordination and diagonal muscle symmetry.

1. Lie on your front with your legs extended, about hip-width apart, and your arms on the floor, bent at the elbows, in the E position. Your forehead can be on the floor or hovering just above it. Imagine that there is a drawing pin underneath your navel. To make sure you do not prick your stomach, activate your pelvic-floor muscle and draw your navel off the mat, scooping your abdominals away from the drawing pin. In the prone position, it generally takes some extra effort to keep your deep abdominals engaged, which you need to do to support the spine properly while you work the back muscles, and also because gravity is working against you. Visualise the crown of your head and your tailbone moving away from each other to create a feeling of length and space in the spine.

2. Breathe in to lift your right arm just an inch or so away from the floor – keep it in its E position, and try to ensure that your hand and your elbow leave the floor at exactly the same time. Breathe out to lower the arm to the mat, replacing the hand and the elbow at precisely the same moment.

3. Breathe in to lift the left arm, and then breathe out as you replace it. Keep alternating arms, and as you lift each one, keep as much space as possible between your shoulder top and your ear lobe to make sure your shoulders don't hunch up. Lift each arm approximately ten times.

4. As you breathe in, lengthen your left leg out of the hip socket – imagine you need to touch something with your big toe just out of reach behind you to create a slight sensation of stretching – and then lift it just an inch or so off the floor. Breathe out to lower the leg.

5. Breathe in to lengthen and then lift your right leg out of the hip socket and then breathe out to lower. You can squeeze your bottom as you lengthen and lift each leg – feel the hamstring muscles at the back of your thigh activate to initiate the lift.

> ### Note
> - It is important to maintain the lengthening feeling just prior to lifting the leg. This is a very precise and controlled movement, and should not cause the pelvis to move. If you find the pelvis is rocking or rolling, increase the engagement of your pelvic-floor muscle and TA as well as squeezing your waist muscles to stabilise the trunk and reduce the range of motion in the leg. When pelvic stability is re-established, you can work on increasing the range of movement of the leg.

exercise continues ➡

Swimming arms.

Swimming legs.

NEXT STEPS

Swimming with Legs and Arms Together

This coordinates the movement of arms and legs in diagonal pairs.

1. Lie in the same starting position as for the basic Swimming exercise. Breathe in to lift your right arm, and lengthen and lift your left leg at the same time. Breathe out to lower.

2. Breathe in to lift your left arm, and lengthen and lift your right leg. Breathe out to lower. Watch out for any rolling or shifting of the ribcage or pelvis – the trunk should stay stable throughout this cross-patterning exercise.

Swimming with Legs and Arms Together.

ADVANCED

Swimming with Arms and Legs Extended

1. Lie in the same starting position as for the basic swimming exercise but this time extend your arms above your head along the floor, palms facing down. The shoulder blades should be gently drawn together and downwards towards the base of the spine to keep the feeling of space and length between your ears and your shoulders.

2. Breathe in to lengthen and lift one arm and the opposite leg off the floor – reach right through your little finger.

3. As you breathe out, lower your arm and leg and simultaneously lengthen and lift your other arm and opposite leg off the floor.

4. Breathe in to lower this diagonal pair, at the same time lengthening and lifting the opposite diagonal pair. Keep this pattern continuously flowing for approximately twenty lifts, concentrating on maintaining pelvic and ribcage stability. Remember to keep lengthening each diagonal pair as it lifts, reaching through the little fingers and through the leg out of the hip socket.

Swimming with Arms and Legs Extended.

NEXT STEPS

Dart

1. Lie on your stomach with your forehead on, or hovering just above, the floor and your arms by your sides with your palms facing the ceiling. Imagine that the drawing pin is still just beneath your navel – keep the abdominals scooped up away from the point. Your bottom and legs should be squeezed together and your toes softly pointed. Draw your shoulder blades back and down as you lengthen the crown of your head and tailbone away from each other. Imagine your headlights are shining directly down towards the floor.

exercise continues ➔

2. Breathe in, and as you breathe out, lengthen and lift your sternum, keeping your neck in line with your spine – think of cradling a peach between your chin and collarbones. This moves the headlight beam forward and up towards the wall. Stretch your arms back and lift them a couple of inches off the floor. Imagine someone has placed their hands on your mid back – engage the spine extensors and latissimus dorsi to push up against their hands. Breathe in to hold this position, and then breathe out to move your headlight beam down towards the floor underneath your chest. Repeat this exercise three more times.

Starting position for Dart.

Extending into Dart.

ADVANCED

Swan

1. Lie on your stomach with your elbows bent and close to your sides, forearms and palms on the floor. Your forehead should hover just off the floor – keep your shoulder tops down away from your ears and the crown of the head lengthening away from your tailbone. Your legs can either be together and gently squeezed, or about hip-width apart. Make sure there is equal pressure in your left and right arms, left and right sides of the pelvis, and left and right legs. Centre your energy and support your lower back by lifting the pelvic-floor muscle and drawing in your navel towards your spine. Concentrate on keeping maximum length through your spine throughout the exercise. Keeping your hips glued to the mat, imagine your headlight beam is shining directly down towards the floor.

2 Breathe in, and as you breathe out, slowly start to move the beam forwards and up to shine on the wall in front of you, peeling your sternum off the floor. Your upper body will start to resemble a ship's figurehead – or a Sphinx. We will call this the Sphinx position.

3. With your elbows and forearm still in contact with the floor, inhale, and as you exhale, slowly move your headlight beam down and along the floor back to the original position.

4. Repeat the exercise, but this time, as you peel the sternum and upper body off the floor, really stretch your legs out to the wall behind you – feel them activate so they start to lift off the floor from your hips. Draw in your navel even more, and squeeze your bottom. Your body will look like a banana, curved off the floor with your feet and sternum reaching away from each other. Inhale, and as you exhale, slowly return your legs and upper body to the mat at the same time. If you are comfortable with extending your spine into the Sphinx position, move on to the next stage.

5. You can either stop in the Sphinx position and, on an out breath, continue into Swan; or use one continuous movement from the start of the exercise. Inhale, and as you exhale, lengthen and lift both legs from the hips – remember to scoop your abdominals up and in, and squeeze your bottom – and simultaneously move your headlight beam farther and farther across the floor and upwards to peel the sternum up.

6. Start to straighten your arms so that only your hands are in contact with the floor. If you can, straighten your arms fully, keeping your shoulder blades drawn back and down. If you can't manage this, straighten as much as is comfortable.

7. Inhale to hold the position – projecting the crown of your head and your tail-bone in opposite directions – and as you exhale, slowly bend your elbows and lower your upper body and legs to the mat to rest in the original position. Repeat three times.

exercise continues ➡

> **Note**
> - This exercise involves intensive work for the low back and it should be included only after you have done several others in neutral spine and spinal flexion. You must stretch the back after doing this exercise.

Starting position for Swan.

Moving into Sphinx, with legs extended.

Full Swan.

Don't tip the head back like this because it puts strain on the neck.

NEXT STEPS
Single-leg Kick

This exercise strengthens the hamstrings and is helpful for improving your ability to apply unilateral leg aids, that is on one side only, while maintaining the stability of the trunk.

1. Lie prone with your upper body in the Sphinx position. Feel your legs lengthening out of the hip sockets – stretch back as if you are trying to touch something behind you with your toes.

2. Activate your leg muscles so that the legs want to lift off the floor. As you breathe in, sharply but smoothly kick your left heel towards your bottom so the lower leg is perpendicular. Do this twice. There's no need to return your leg towards the floor between kicks – three or four inches is sufficient. Lower the leg towards the floor as you breathe out. Keep lengthening the leg out of the hip socket.

3. Breathe in to kick the right leg sharply but smoothly towards your bottom and then breathe out to lower the leg towards the floor.

4. Repeat approximately ten times on each side, using your legs alternately.

> *Note*
> - The kicks should be controlled and performed in a clockwork rhythm.
>
> - After this exercise, it is important to stretch out your back and hamstring muscles. Use Child's Pose or Cat Stretch and Spine Stretch or Roll Down for this.

exercise continues ➡

The starting position for Single-leg Kick is Sphinx.

Kick one leg towards the bottom.

NEXT STEPS

Double-leg Kick

This exercise helps you to improve your ability to apply bilateral leg aids, that is both sides at once, while maintaining trunk stability. It is virtually the same as the Single-leg Kick except that instead of moving the legs alternately, both legs kick towards the bottom at the same time.

1. Lie in the Sphinx position as before and activate your leg muscles so that the legs want to lift off the floor.

2. Breathe in and kick both heels sharply but with control towards your bottom twice. Breathe out as you lower them towards the floor.

Note

- Keep the pelvis absolutely stable – the navel should be drawn right away from the mat.

- Focus on maintaining the same distance between your heels as they move away from the floor.

- Your lower legs should be perpendicular – they should not move inwards towards your spine.

- Along with your back muscles, your hamstring muscles should be stretched after performing this exercise. Use Child's Pose or Cat Stretch and Spine Stretch or Roll Down.

The starting position for Double-leg Kick is Sphinx.

Kick both legs towards the bottom.

Stretching back muscles

All exercises in the prone position work your back muscles, which must be stretched out afterwards. Take up Child's Pose or Cat Stretch immediately after Swimming, Dart, Swan, Single- or Double-leg Kick.

Child's Pose

1. From the prone position, push yourself up on to all fours and then sit on your heels.

2. Widen your knees a little and lower your chest and forehead to the floor, arms by your feet with your palms turned up towards the ceiling. Hold this position for around twenty seconds.

> *Note*
> • If this is uncomfortable for your knees or you can't get your chest low enough to the floor to feel much of a stretch in your back, use Cat Stretch instead.

Child's Pose.

Cat Stretch

1. From the prone position, push yourself up on to all fours with your weight equally distributed between your knees and hands. Make sure your knees are directly below your hips and your hands are directly below your shoulders.

2. In a neutral spine position with your pelvic-floor muscle and TA engaged, breathe in and as you breathe out, move the crown of your head and your tailbone towards each other as if they are going to meet underneath you. Imagine someone has tied a string to your belt and it is being pulled up towards the ceiling. As your spine moves into flexion, you should feel a good stretch in the back muscles you have just been working. Take care that the weight distribution on your four points is not disturbed at all.

3. When the crown of your head and tailbone are as close as possible, breathe in and allow them to separate as you move back into neutral spine. Do not hyperextend your spine.

4. Repeat this three more times, moving the spine into flexion as you exhale, and returning it to neutral as you inhale.

Cat Stretch.

Chapter **10**

Structuring Your Programme

A Pilates session should consist of a warm-up, workout and cool-down.

Why warm up?

Warming up in the right way is important before undertaking any type of exercise. I often ask new students how long they usually take to warm up their horses before starting the main part of their schooling session, whether that be flat work or jumping. Answers range between ten and twenty minutes. When I ask the same riders how long they take to warm up themselves before riding, I am often met with blank expressions and a slightly surprised or bashful, 'I don't.'

As a rider myself, I am aware that we often tend to be short of time, and fit rides in quickly before or after work, or slotted into the busy routine of the rest of the day. However, riding is an occupation of quality rather than quantity. Many hours in the saddle are required to build up skills and expertise, but practising wrongly is just as unhelpful as not practising at all! You can offer a horse a better standard of riding if you take a few minutes before mounting him to concentrate on your own body.

Incorporating a few simple flexibility exercises into your horsey routine before you ride will mobilise the spine in the same way as you expect it to function while you are in the saddle, and therefore reduce the possibility of potential injury and possible aches and pains. A carefully considered warm-up also increases your body's ability to keep your boxes stacked correctly, and the more accurately you are able to stack your boxes, the clearer the communication with your horse will be, and the better the riding experience for both of you. Taking a moment to focus on your alignment, your balance, breathing and centring your-self should set the scene for a positive ride. Your joints are required to absorb a significant amount of shock from the motion of the horse, and postural as well as global muscles have quite some work to do to stabilise your position and apply aids. No one would dream of attempting an aerobic workout, five-mile run or gym session without warming up adequately to avoid the possibility of injury, yet many people hop on board their horses without a second thought.

I must also point out that warming up is particularly important in colder weather. It is frustrating to spend the majority of your ride battling against stiff-ness and lack of fluidity in your own body due to low temperatures or a biting wind. By the time you have loosened up enough to work productively, the ride is probably nearly over.

The following warm-up consists of standing exercises. It is intended for use as preparation for your ridden work and can be performed in the stable or tack room. However, it includes all the components of a pre-Pilates workout, so you can use it for that purpose. Cold, tight muscles are damaged easily – warming up properly will ensure your Pilates practice is beneficial.

above left A dressage rider warming up before a competition – in the snow! Roll Down …

above centre Side Stretch…

above right Sundial.

Standing warm-up exercises

First, march up and down on the spot for thirty seconds. Then do each of the following movements on an out breath, and remember to engage your pelvic-floor muscle and TA throughout.

- Neck mobilisation – stand with your feet hip-width apart, weight central. Lengthen your spine, pull up your pelvic-floor muscle and pull in your TA.

- Curl your chin to your chest and then restack to neutral. Do this four times.

- Turn your head to look over each shoulder twice

- Tilt your head sideways, twice each side

- Shoulder mobilisation – circle your shoulders slowly and smoothly up, back and down. Do this eight times. There is no need to circle your shoulders forwards since most people's shoulders come forwards too much anyway.

- Cleopatra, four times

- Side Stretch, twice on each side, for spinal flexion

- Stand on one leg and then the other leg for four seconds each

- Bow or sternum float twice, for spinal flexion and extension

- Roll Downs, four times, for spinal flexion

- Sundial twice each way, for spinal rotation

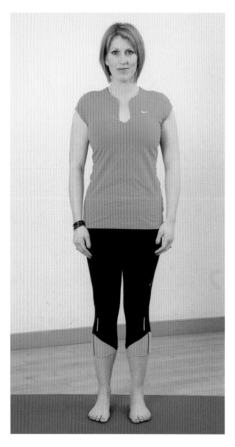

Neck mobilisation.

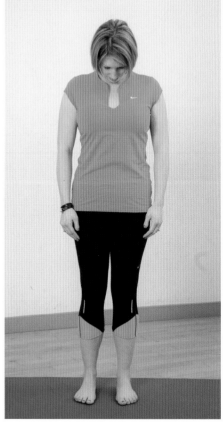

Chin curl.

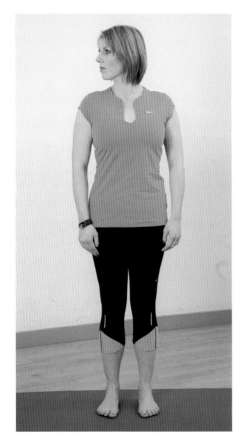 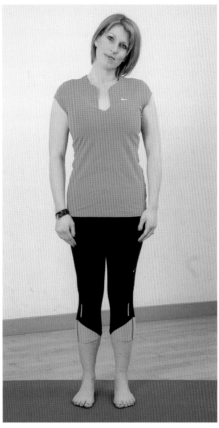

left-hand photo Head turn.

right-hand photo Head tilt.

Pre-ride micro warm-up

This takes a couple of minutes, so even if you haven't time for the full warm-up, there is no excuse for not doing this one – your horse will thank you for your efforts.

- Roll Downs, four times
- Side Stretches, two each way
- Sundial, two each way

The workout

Ideally, your Pilates practice should involve a mixture of exercises in different positions – standing, semi-supine, side-lying, sitting and prone. This is the most effective way to improve general spinal flexibility, and it also challenges your core stability.

To feel a real and lasting improvement, you need to carry out a structured Pilates workout of around forty-five minutes to an hour twice a week. If you have that time available and can commit to a regular routine, brilliant. However, if that is not realistic for you – and many other things can, understandably, take priority – don't worry because there is a practical alternative. Don't fall into the trap of thinking that if you don't have an hour to spare, there is no point in doing anything. A mini-workout of ten to fifteen minutes carried out on five to seven days a week is much less daunting than having to find a whole hour, and can be just as effective.

The actual workout is not the only exercise that helps to re-educate your body. Remember to notice the little things – how you stand when you brush your teeth, how your weight is distributed when you drive your car, how you walk. Applying the principles of Pilates, and in particular the ABC – alignment, breathing, centring – to your daily routine can make big changes, too.

For a full, hour-long workout, you need to include either the standing or intermediate warm-up before practising your main exercise selection. For a mini workout, use the micro warm-up and also use this as a cool-down. The full standing warm-up can even count as one of your mini-workouts.

I have included three sample full workouts in this chapter, one for a beginner, one for an intermediate-level session and one more advanced. However, I would encourage you to design your own session plans, using the guide given at the end. Try to put together three or four different ones for your current level of working, which you can use in rotation. Plenty of variety stops you getting bored with your practice, and working to your own plans gives an added sense of achievement as you improve. Re-visiting a workout plan a little while after first using it helps you to measure your progress, and to see if you feel confident enough to increase the challenge of any exercise to the next level.

For full workouts, select about four of the semi-supine position exercises, and two each of the side-lying, sitting and prone exercises. For a mini workout, choose about three semi-supine exercises and one each of the side-lying, sitting and prone. Carefully read each description of the exercises; your plan needs to move the spine in flexion, lateral flexion, rotation and extension.

Cool-down

The cool-down section of the practice is important to make sure you stretch the muscles worked during the session in order to avoid delayed onset muscle soreness (DOMS) – you know that dreadful aching you get in your inner thighs after riding having had a break from it? Careful stretching of muscles after working them helps to avoid that aching feeling.

It is also helpful to stretch muscle groups that tend to tighten up because of how they're used while riding. Over time, tightness in these muscles affects their ability to function properly, which can hinder your riding progress as well as cause discomfort. The nature of the Pilates exercises detailed in this book means that many of those muscle groups are actually lengthened during the workout, but additional stretches are still beneficial. Those that follow can be incorporated in your cool-down. All of these stretches should be held for a minimum of twenty seconds to be of benefit – they should be held steadily and not 'bounced'.

Hip-flexor stretch

Stand with your feet hip-width apart, then stride forwards with your left leg and lower your hips towards the floor – keep your spine in neutral and your abdominals engaged. Make sure your left knee stays above your ankle and does not push beyond the toe. Push your pelvis lower and at the same time float your arms into a V position above your head, lengthening the front of your body – if you feel any pressure in the lower back, draw your navel in and lower your tailbone to the floor behind you. You should feel a fairly intensive stretch in the right hip. Repeat on the other leg.

Hip-flexor stretch.

Quadriceps stretch

Stand facing a wall and using your right hand on the wall for support, stand on your right leg and take hold of your left ankle with your left hand. Keeping your boxes stacked and your pelvic-floor muscle and TA engaged – no twisting, tilting or shifting of the pelvis or ribcage – draw the thigh back until your knees are together and you feel a distinctive stretch in the front of the thigh. Repeat, this time standing on your left leg and stretching the right thigh muscles.

Quadriceps stretch.

Calf stretch

This targets both muscles in the calf. They act to draw your heels upwards. To stretch the gastrocnemius muscle, stand facing a wall about three feet away and take a step forward with your left foot. Place both hands on the wall in front of you with your elbows slightly bent and all your boxes stacked and directly facing the wall. Keeping your right leg straight, slowly bend your left knee until you feel the stretch in your right calf muscle, keeping both heels on the ground.

To stretch the other calf muscle in your right leg, the soleus, continue the exercise by slowly bending your right knee, ensuring your right heel stays on the

Gastrocnemius stretch.

ground. Slowly push yourself back to starting position. Then take your left leg back and right leg forward to repeat the straight knee and bent knee stretches on your left leg.

Hip-abductor stretch

This is better described as the TFL/IT band stretch, a deeper version of the side stretch, targeting the abductor muscles of the hip in addition to the upper body. TFL stands for tensor fascia lata, which is part of the hip abductor muscle group and also of the hip medial rotator group. The tendinous ilio-tibial (IT) band stretches from the outer hip to the side of the knee.

Imagine you are standing in a doorway. Cross your left leg in front of your right leg. Float your right arm up towards the ceiling and curve it over your head – imagine reaching for the left side of the door frame. Put your left hand on your hip and push slightly to move your hips to the right. As you continue to hold the stretch, you will feel a lengthening on the outer torso, hip, upper thigh and knee of your right leg. You can make the stretch more intensive by placing your feet a little farther apart, bending the knee of your forward foot and keeping the back knee straight.

Repeat, crossing your right leg in front of your left leg and floating your left arm up and over as you push the hips left to stretch the left TFL and IT band.

Hip-abductor stretch.

Hamstring stretch

Hamstring imbalances can cause the pelvis to rotate on the femur, making it hard to sit straight with your legs positioned evenly in the saddle. The Roll Down and Spine Stretch with legs extended exercises provide a hamstring stretch. I also like to use the following stretches as they target the inner and outer thigh. You will need a stretch band. These are inexpensive and widely available from sports shops and online.

Lie on your back with your knees bent. Take your stretch band and place it around the toes and ball of your left foot, leaving an inch of band visible beyond your big toe. Straighten your left leg and push through your heel, bringing it up towards the ceiling and towards you. Make sure your knee is straight before lifting the leg. Keep you elbows on the floor and shorten the band until you feel mild discomfort in the hamstrings at the back of the leg. Hold for a minimum of twenty seconds.

Bring the leg out away from the centre, knee straight and push through your heel with the leg as close to the ground as possible. Hold for a minimum of twenty seconds.

Bring the leg over to the right (this will probably be harder) and, pushing through the heel, hold for a minimum of twenty seconds. Repeat with the other leg. To make the stretch more intensive, extend the non-stretching leg.

above Hamstring stretch using a stretch band.
right Extending the leg on the floor makes the stretch more intensive. *below left* Stretching the inner thigh.
below right Stretching the outer thigh.

Piriformis stretch

Lie on your back and cross your right leg over your left – thigh over thigh. Hold your ankles and gently pull them towards you and apart a little – you will feel the stretch in the outside of your right thigh, at the top. Repeat, crossing your left leg over your right to feel the stretch at the top and outside of your left leg.

Piriformis stretch.

Gluteus-maximus stretch

Lie on your back and cross your right ankle over your left knee. Now reach forward to grasp the back of your left thigh with both hands and pull it towards your chest until you feel a stretch in your bottom. Repeat, this time crossing your left ankle over your right knee and grasping the back of your right thigh.

Gluteus-maximus stretch.

Inner-thigh stretch

This targets the adductor muscles. Sit with your legs in the prayer position (soles of feet touching) and then bring your ankles closer to you. Gently press your elbows on to your knees to push them a little farther towards the floor until you feel a stretch in the inner thighs.

Inner thigh stretch.

Sample workouts

Beginner

Warm-up:
Do the full standing warm-up described on pages 175–176. This should take 10–15 minutes.

Workout:
Semi-supine exercises:
Single-arm Floats, twice with each arm
Double-arm Floats, twice with each arm
Leg Slides
Pelvic Tilts, four
Shoulder Bridge, four
Hip and Head Roll, four each way

Side-lying exercises:

Side Kick (levels one and two), both sides

Prone exercises:

Swimming, arms only, in E position

Swimming, legs only

Child's Pose

Sitting exercise:

Spine Twist

Cool-down:

Spine Stretch

Roll Downs

Side Stretch with TFL/IT band stretch

Quadriceps stretch

Shoulder rolls

Head turns, tilts and rolls

Intermediate

Warm-up:

Start in semi-supine position and activate the pelvic-floor muscle and TA

Arm Floats, four with each arm

Leg Slides, four with each leg

Toy-soldier Arm Floats and Leg Slides

Head floats, four – maintain space between chin and chest; lift your head
    an inch from the floor as you exhale, inhale to lower.

Head turns, four

Head tilts, four

Pelvic tilt, four

Hip and Head Roll, four each way

Workout:

Leg Floats to tabletop, eight each leg

Leg Floats with Circles, four each leg

Shoulder Bridge, four, with heel raise on final two

Side Kick, levels three and four (if appropriate), left side

Swimming, in E position, legs and arms together for 20 strokes

Dart

Child's Pose or Cat Stretch

Side Kick, levels three and four (if appropriate), right side
Half-seated Roll Back
Spine Twist, four each way

Cool-down:
Spine Stretch
Piriformis stretch
Chest Opener
Full body stretch – lie on your back, legs straight and arms on the floor above
    your head

Advanced

Warm-up:
Do the full standing warm-up described on pages 175–176.

Workout:
Single-leg Floats to tabletop, two each leg
Double-leg Floats to tabletop, four each leg
Toe Taps, four each leg
Pelvic Roll, four each way
Shoulder Bridge, six, with leg extension on final two
Roll Up, six
Spine Twist, full position, four each way
Side Kick, level four, left side
Swan, four
Single-leg Kick, four each leg
Child's Pose/Cat Stretch
Side Kick, level four, right side

Cool-down:
Hip and Head Roll, two each way
Hamstring stretches with band
Gluteus-maximus stretch
Piriformis stretch
TFL/IT band standing stretch
Quadriceps stretch
Calf stretch

Conclusion

Your body is the harp of your soul, as it is yours to bring forth from it sweet music or confused sounds.

KHALIL GIBRAN (Lebanese American artist and poet, 1883–1931)

I love this quote – it resonates with me because through Pilates I have been able to tune my body considerably. Through developing my own interpretation and application of the techniques and principles of Joseph Pilates – my approach is known as Equipilates – I have been able to help many riders achieve remarkable progress. I continue to learn each day as clients present new levels of subtlety in how they and their horses interact, and also from the complexities of the relationships with my own horses.

I hope that the Pilates exercises, tension-release techniques and approach to body awareness in this book will help your riding to the extent that you can really communicate on a deep, subtle and technically accurate level with your horse. There are no useful shortcuts on the road to riding excellence – it is not a race, but a journey of personal development, and all too often we are left fumbling in the dark, wondering which route to follow. However, correcting your spinal alignment, releasing unnecessary tension, increasing the core support for your spine, and applying the principles of Pilates in your everyday life, and every time you put your foot into the stirrup, are all steps in the right direction. The Pilates map is definitely the best I have found.

Recommended Reading

Anatomy of Dressage, Heinrich Schusdziarra and Volker Schusdziarra

A Search for Collection: Science and Art in Riding, Paul Belasik

Dressage Formula, Erik Herbermann

Elements of Dressage, Kurd Albrecht von Ziegner

Exploring Dressage Technique, Paul Belasik

Real Life Dressage, Carl Hester and Polly Ellison

Riding Towards The Light, Paul Belasik

School of Horsemanship, François Robichon de la Guérinière

The Competitive Edge III: Gravity, Balance & Kinetics of the Horse & Rider, Max Gahwyler

The Equine Psoas Manual, Joanne Greenfield

The Gymnasium of the Horse, Gustav Steinbrecht

The Psoas Book, Liz Koch

Tug of War, Gerd Heuschmann

Twisted Truths of Modern Dressage, Philippe Karl

Index